DIVINE DESIGN

Created for Relationship with God in Order to Be on Mission with God

Dwight Smith

Formatting by Reddovedesign.com
Funded and produced by BookRally:

www.bookrally.com

CONTENTS

PREFACE

"Why did you write this book, and who is the audience?" I have been asked that many times by publishers and editors. And every time, I hesitate, and I ponder. Why did I spend the last twenty years pondering the thoughts in this book? Why did I record note after note along my journey, responding each time to a new thought or discovery that the Spirit of God was speaking into my life? I guess in essence I wrote this book because I wanted to record for myself and those close to me the discoveries that I believed God was teaching me that made the walk He has called me to more joyous, more satisfying, and, I hope, more effective as I have sought to live and declare His glory. Who is the audience? I am!

I am the intended audience, because in these chapters you will find my own struggle to live as fully as possible in the center of God-provided meaning, significance, and service with joy and satisfaction. The things you will read come from my own understanding of Scripture as I have consistently spent time in it, seeking to obey all that God has created us to become and do.

But, obviously, the fact that you have found this book means that there is also a greater audience: you, the faithful follower of Jesus Christ! My wife and I have been privileged to minister the gospel with people from all over the world—over seventy countries at last count!—and while we are more often than not joyfully surprised (again and again) by the faithfulness we see in many of Christ's followers, we are also perplexed—no, alarmed—at the lives that so many are living.

The most alarming are those who say that they are Jesus followers but show no signs of the life that being a follower of Christ anticipates. They appear to me, in my limited view of what is inside them, to be stillborn. Life was apparently in them at the moment of a confession, but when brought to the light of day and the regimen of living life on a daily basis, they prove to be dead.

I know that some will say to me, "You are not God—you don't know what's in their hearts." Absolutely I am not God. And I must admit that I do not fully understand the conflict that these believers experience. But I am one called to call others to walk with God, accessing daily His Word, listening to the Holy Spirit, and obeying and bending into the designs of God rather than their flesh. As such, I never want to assume that confession without fruit constitutes a guarantee of eternity with God. Indeed, the opposite seems to be the clearly repeated biblical message.

Equally perplexing to me are those who say that they are Jesus followers but continue to struggle with issues for which the Bible has answers, healing, and an ever-increasing life of maturation. As the writer of Hebrews so clearly says, let's move on from the basics: "Let us leave the elementary doctrine of Christ and go on to maturity" (Heb. 6:1). Indeed some of the "elementary" things that he mentions in the verses following this one would strike many of us as significant issues of faith. And they are. But God is compelling His people to step over these threshold issues and move on—to move on to a walk with God that rejects the flesh and more consistently understands the difference between good and evil.

This issue of moving on in the faith is so important that the writer gives us a simple analogy to show its power, its reasonable expectation: "Land that has drunk the rain that often falls on it, and produces a crop useful to those for whose sake it is cultivated, receives a blessing from God. But if it bears thorns and thistles, it is worthless and near to being cursed, and its end is to be burned" (Heb. 6:7–8).

Even as I reflect on this preface, I realize more fully that my purpose in writing this book is to demonstrate to readers from God's Word that maturity in the faith is not unusual, nor is it negotiable. It is expected. Indeed, it is the design of God for those who have been born again in Jesus Christ. It need not be a follow-on experience of growth in the Spirit. We can enter into relationship with God through the threshold of faith and continue growing, just as a seed naturally reproduces, just as God has designed things to be.

Just as importantly, I want Christians to understand that I am not writing about some new form of discipleship. In fact, when it comes to any curriculum or program we dub "discipleship," if the teaching of Scripture doesn't take root and multiply in our lives, our curriculum is useless.

Nearly fifty years of service to the body of Christ have taught me that these things that rise from new birth are as natural as the air we breathe and meant to multiply as inherently as the good seed that falls into fertile ground and produces much fruit. God has designed righteousness for His people. And He will grow it in us. Ours is to realize it, ponder it, and submit to the spiritual disciplines necessary to see God the Spirit grow it.

I have struggled to know how best to communicate this message to a present generation. As my wife and I read through the manuscript, we immediately remembered people who have most demonstrated a particular expression of what I am writing, and I felt urged to include their stories. But I chose to do little storytelling, for three reasons.

One, I am a lousy storyteller.

Two, too many Christians identify with a story but have no concept about what it took for a person to actually live the story and then to give testimony to its result. We have become like people who want chocolate ice cream but don't want to know, much less be responsible for, the actions it took to prepare the ice cream. We hear a great story and want to experience it ourselves, but that story cost somebody something. Indeed, it may have cost that person a lot of things for a long period of time before the appealing fruit of the story actually came to fruition in his or her life. God does not give us chocolate ice cream without our full participation in the process.

Finally, I believe that ultimately God speaks to our wills. Yes, He has given us an inspired Word to feed our minds, and He has given us emotions to feel, both pain as well as joy. But He is most concerned about what we do with what we know, which many times requires us to say no to our emotions that are so easily dominated by the flesh. We need to be people who are willing to spend the time and effort to think!

So if you are hoping that this book will be easy to read, or that it will lead to your greatest day ever, or that the small seed of money you have invested into a particular ministry will harvest of a miraculous amount of goods for you, or that you want to speak against a particular sickness in your body and be guaranteed of a healing, then this book may not be for you.

Hebrews 11 makes it clear to us that God has designed a different obedience experience for each of His children. Some of them have lived wealthy and powerful lives. Others of them "suffered mocking and flogging, and even chains and imprisonment. They were stoned, they were sawn in two, they were killed with the sword. They went about in skins of sheep and goats, destitute, afflicted, mistreated—of whom the world was not worthy—wandering about in deserts and mountains, and in dens and caves of the earth" (Heb. 11:36–38).

But each of them believed God and were "rewarded" for their faith:

These all died in faith, not having received the things promised, but having seen them and greeted them from afar, and having acknowledged that they were strangers and exiles on the earth. For people who speak thus make it clear that they are seeking a homeland. If they had been thinking of that land from which they had gone out, they would have had opportunity to return. But as it is, they desire a better country, that is, a heavenly one.

Therefore God is not ashamed to be called their God, for he has prepared for them a city. (Heb. 11:13–16)

If you are a believer in Christ who wants to move on from the threshold of faith, on to a life full of the designs of God for you, then this is the book you want to read. It will call you to read Scripture more regularly, ponder what the Spirit is saying to you, and bend your will to the will of your Father! Through this He will form His righteousness in you, and you will know joy—His joy—and fulfillment. This is His design for you.

introduction

GOD'S MISSION—AND OUR PART IN IT

Whatever God is going to do in the world, He is going to do primarily through all Christ's people. God is on mission—*missio Dei*—and He calls every believer in Christ to partner with Him in His work in our scattered locations as we live and speak the gospel.

Too often in the twentieth and twenty-first centuries we have seen pastors, leaders, missionaries, and others in ministry doing the work of God, while the ordinary believer is occupied or even entertained with an abundance of contemporary church programs. But this model is far from the plan of God in the creation of man. Each individual is created with a purpose, a divine design, and intended to play an active role in God's mercy mission.

While this idea may sound foreign to some Western readers, I am amazed at how natural it sounds to countless church leaders in the many nations where I have been privileged to minister. Why is it so natural sounding to them? I hope it is because they instinctively understand the potential gospel power of millions of Christ's people distributed daily in all the marketplaces[1] and locales where God intends to reveal Himself through His people's lives, choices, and witness.

This truth that God intends to use all His people for His mission in this world is a promise from Scripture—a promise that declares God's design for His people: "We are his workmanship, created in Christ Jesus for good works, which God prepared beforehand, that we should walk in them" (Eph. 2:10). This promise, however, comes with an imperative: you and I, as believers in Jesus Christ, have to believe it, embrace it, and act on it by living incarnational lives among the people and in the places where God has put us.

The gospel we are called to live out is centered upon mercy, which flows unilaterally from God through Christ to a world He created to commune with Him but that now exists in rebellion to Him. As we receive that mercy by embracing the gospel, we are re-created by the Spirit into sanctified human instruments and transformed—re-created out of the sinful life we inherited from the first Adam into the new life of the last Adam, Jesus Christ. As Romans 6 so explicitly declares, we are crucified, buried, and resurrected with Jesus Christ into newness of life—life to God! This is the life God designed us to live from the beginning.

As I have grown in my understanding of the role of God's people in the world and interacted with believers who cooperate fully with God and His gospel regarding this mission, I have increasingly seen both the simplicity and the depth of these truths.

They are simple, because the storyline of the Bible is not complicated. I have a small wristband with five symbols on it intended to tell the story of the gospel, and as I have rehearsed what I will say when asked about the wristband, I have told myself the simple Bible story from beginning to end: all have sinned; Jesus' blood covers our sin; we are washed white as snow; God gives us new life; and we have the hope of heaven. The gospel is the centerpiece to the Bible's storyline.

But these truths are also deep, because our personal salvation message is not the whole story! When we begin asking, "Where does the story actually begin?" we discover the divine design revealed in the Genesis creation story, and it affects who we are as followers of Jesus today. See, as followers of Christ, you and I are the abiding place of the Holy Spirit, and we now have the fruit of the Spirit (see Gal. 5:22–23) flowing through us and out of us. Because of this fruit, we increasingly learn to relate to people differently than we could have when we were dominated by flesh, sin, and self-centeredness. But these Christlike characteristics working in and through us are true and real and alive— because they are how God designed things to be in the beginning. They are also reflections of how things will be at the end of time, in the eternity of a new heaven and a new earth. This is divine design:

> *[God] chose us in [Christ] before the foundation of the world, that we should be holy and blameless before him. In love he predestined us for adoption as sons through Jesus Christ, according to the purpose of his will, to the praise of his glorious grace, with which he has blessed us in the Beloved. In him we have redemption through his blood, the forgiveness of our trespasses, according to the riches of his grace, which he lavished upon us, in all wisdom and insight making known to us the mystery of his will, according to his purpose, which he set forth in Christ as a plan for the fullness of time, to unite all things in him, things in heaven and things on earth. (Eph. 1:4–10)*

Genesis declares, and the New Testament affirms, that man is designed to eventually serve God in the full restoration of the righteousness in which the Lord first created Adam and Eve. In the meantime, we are to serve God in the mission He is carrying out across human history until the final time of judgment.

The Church in Need of Reformation

In order to accomplish His mercy mission in our era of history, God has created the church and sent us out into the world. His design is that we should impact the people around us in our marketplaces, neighborhoods, and homes.

In the Old Testament God created and designed Israel to be His instrument. Israel was to live in such a way, described in the Mosaic economy, that the nations would be drawn to them, seeing in them a unique people among peoples submitted to, provided by, and blessed by God. Their failure in this design, however, is recorded across the pages of the Old Testament. But as Hebrews 10 declares, they were a symbol, anticipating a day when God would not dwell with His people in a temple but within them:

> *Do you not know that your body is a temple of the Holy Spirit within you, whom you have from God? You are not your own, for you were bought with a price. (1 Cor. 6:19–20)*

> *You are fellow citizens with the saints and members of the household of God, built on the foundation of the apostles and prophets, Christ Jesus himself being the cornerstone, in whom the whole structure, being joined together, grows into a holy temple in the Lord. In him you also are being built together into a dwelling place for God by the Spirit. (Eph. 2:19–22)*

But just as Israel failed to live out God's purpose for them, the church of the twenty-first century wavers in its obedience to God's call of partnership with Him in mission. It was because of this that my wife, Patti, and I founded Saturation Church Planting International in 1995. Over the last twenty years, we have sought to partner with national leaders globally to mobilize the church in order to see the full evangelization of nations around the world through what we call "evangelization through incarnational saturation"—God's people living incarnational lives among the people and in the places where He calls them. In our endeavors we have found thousands of leaders around the world who are drawn into the message we preach of church reformation.

This message is sometimes in tension with what we have learned from some of our Christian fathers over the last several generations. Living in a Christian culture, many of them tended to view the church as a place rather than, as Scripture so clearly declares us to be, a people. We do not seek to criticize or deconstruct what they taught us, but under the secularizing flood of the twentieth and twenty-first centuries that has affected the church at large, we have been driven back to Scripture and have gained a more emphatic understanding of God's Word. As believers in Christ, we are a people temporary to this earth, sent by a merciful God to live and declare His story of grace into all the places He takes us.

Even though these thoughts about the church and completing the task God has left His people in our day appear at times reformational, I have come to see that they were set in God's revelation from the very beginning. They are not a call to something new but rather to conform to divine design—God's original creation of a world of righteousness. This design was marred when Adam and Eve chose personal God-separating disobedience and set into motion the rebellious world we live in today, but this rebellion is not forever—it will last only until the day that God judges the rebellion and creates a new world of righteousness in His intended design.

Despite the fall, God's design is seen clearly in the words of Jesus in the Sermon on the Mount and across the pages of the New Testament. Through Jesus' death, burial, and resurrection, God has restored a righteous likeness of God in the people He created and the world He designed for us to live in. Until He restores it completely upon Jesus' return to Earth, this generation of the church is to live God's righteous values before and in the world—a world He calls to Himself either for salvation or for judgment. These values are the life of Jesus in us, drawn from the life of His Father, reflected by the life of the Holy Spirit in those of us who are followers of Jesus Christ. The Trinity works in harmony to bring this into demonstration in us. This is life as God designed it from the beginning.

Believers in Christ: On Mission with God

The story in the Bible is indeed a simple one. Many teachings from the Bible have been taught by faithful followers of Jesus Christ from past generations, and through them we have gained great insight into biblical truths that needed clarification. Through these spiritual teachers we have gained increasing grounds for unity as we have come to appreciate and affirm our convictions about the triune nature of God, the divinity and equally important humanity of the Son of God, and so many other teachings that we now consider orthodox. Ongoing research and writing by those we call theologians give us greater insight into the composition and preservation of the holy book we call our Bible. To the degree that God designs to be publicly affirmed, ongoing discoveries in archeology, history, geography, and other fields of study ultimately and consistently affirm His creation and sustentation of our planet. While I gladly embrace all the points of doctrine just mentioned, this book is about the simple story of the Bible and how that should be lived out by every believer.

From Genesis to Revelation, we see God acting to bring mercy to the people He made in the place He created for them. God has a mission of redemption to enact across human history until finally the judgment promised in the beginning comes (see Gen. 3:15; 2 Pet. 3:7–10).

God wants to extend His character of mercy to the world, and He wants to do it through those who have been reconciled to Him in Jesus. From the beginning God has designed that those who belong to Him, whether in the Old Testament or New Testament, are to join Him in this mercy task. We who belong to Him were originally designed to join our God in establishing righteousness in creation, and now, after the fall, we are designed to reestablish it, through Jesus, because of our re-creation through the salvation that we have in His life, death, and resurrection:

If anyone is in Christ, he is a new creation. The old has passed away; behold, the new has come. All this is from God, who through Christ reconciled us to himself and gave us the ministry of reconciliation; that is, in Christ God was reconciling the world to himself, not counting their trespasses against them, and entrusting to us the message of reconciliation. Therefore, we are ambassadors for Christ, God making his appeal through us. (2 Cor. 5:17–20)

In order to see people reconciled to God today, the Lord has created the church and sent every believer to join Him in this mission. Believers in Jesus Christ are to tell this story of mercy, as the Lord Himself made clear in Matthew 28:18–20:

All authority in heaven and on earth has been given to me. Go therefore and make disciples of all nations, baptizing them in the name of the Father and of the Son and of the Holy Spirit, teaching them to observe all that I have commanded you. And behold, I am with you always, to the end of the age.

The church is a body of people that is to be radically different from the generation that surrounds it. God Himself took decisive action to bring this body of believers into this world, gave it a solid foundation upon which to live, built into it His own presence, and gave it an eternal purpose. Paul defines the church in Ephesians 3–4 as God's merciful presence in the world in this current era of history.[2]

Over the decades we at Saturation Church Planting have discovered, attempted to live, and trained others in this miraculous creation of God in Christ's people. Over that time we have been driven deeper into reflection and further into Scripture and have found that the principles we see so clearly in the New Testament do not stand alone as church belief only. Indeed, they are indications of the one storyline of the Bible—that God is unilaterally acting in mercy, through His Son

Jesus Christ, to restore His creation, both spiritually and physically, to Himself. For those of us who belong to Him, living this gospel message is to be the central focus of our lives.

As the New Testament so clearly states, we are to do this by telling our own mercy experience (see Eph. 3:10–11). We are to daily use the gifts of the Spirit, who lives in us, in all our relationships and vocations (see 1 Cor. 12:4–11). We are to mature in the fruit of the new life that God has placed in us through salvation in His Son, Jesus Christ (see Gal. 5:22–23). We are to mature in stewarding the assets that God places in our hands in order to actively cooperate with God's mercy story (see 1 Tim. 6:17–19). These behaviors, among others that we will consider later, reflect the divine design being lived in and through us.

These qualities impact the sum total of our lives. They affect the way we view our individual lives and their meaning, purpose, and worth. They impact the way we view our marriages and their strategic importance not only to the oneness that results in children or togetherness with another person but to the purpose God has designed for these unions to demonstrate His glory. They impact how we order our lives, what we do with our money, how we transact business, how we pursue one vocation over another, what we think about retirement, and, ultimately, how we address the certainty of death.

Though the progressive revelation of the Bible has made the manifold design of God clearer through New Testament teaching and, more importantly, through the life and teaching of God's final Word, Jesus Christ, this design is not new. It is the design God planned from the very beginning!

That is the focus of this book—to demonstrate that things like evangelism and discipleship are not new topics any more than they are add-on programs to the life of a local church. Life as God designed it and as Jesus demonstrated it begins in Genesis 1 and is fully restored in Revelation 22. God has a simple and singular story in the Bible: He created us for Himself and, therefore, for righteousness in thought and action.

Adam failed the first offer of this design; however, Jesus, the last Adam, restored its potential. Therefore, all of us who are found in the last Adam are restored to this original design. One day, life after death will bring about the complete restoration to this design. On a new earth, breathing the air of a new heaven, and living as citizens of a new Jerusalem, we will eternally experience all that God intended for Adam and Eve and all that they rejected:

> *I saw a new heaven and a new earth, for the first heaven and the first earth had passed away, and the sea was no more. And I saw the holy city, new Jerusalem, coming down out of heaven from God, prepared as a bride adorned for her husband. And I heard a loud voice from the throne saying, "Behold, the dwelling place of God is with man. He will dwell with them, and they will be his people, and God himself will be with them as their God."* (Rev. 21:1–3)

However, while we are here on this earth, we are to live out and proclaim this message of mercy:

> *Since all these things are thus to be dissolved, what sort of people ought you to be in lives of holiness and godliness, waiting for and hastening the coming of the day of God, because of which the heavens will be set on fire and dissolved, and the heavenly bodies will melt as they burn! But according to his promise we are waiting for new heavens and a new earth in which righteousness dwells.* (2 Pet. 3:11–13)

We are to live our lives, the sum total of them, as people who know the end of the story.

This book is an attempt to show that the beginning of God's story is equally as important as the end and sets in place the seed for understanding the whole story. God has graciously offered to heal mankind's rebellion and build a new life in us—the life of righteousness He designed at creation but is now seen most clearly seen in His Son, Jesus Christ. This is the message we must hear, embrace, and act on so that we can fulfill God's call to be on mission with Him as He works to restore creation to Himself.

PART ONE

Divine Design in the Beginning

Then God said, "Let us make man in our image, after our likeness. And let them have dominion over the fish of the sea and over the birds of the heavens and over the livestock and over all the earth and over every creeping thing that creeps on the earth." So God created man in his own image, in the image of God he created him; male and female he created them. And God blessed them. And God said to them, "Be fruitful and multiply and fill the earth and subdue it, and have dominion over the fish of the sea and over the birds of the heavens and over every living thing that moves on the earth."

Genesis 1:26–28

chapter 1

DIVINE DESIGN REVEALED

The Bible tells the story of human history—or, better yet, the story of God working in human history. In Genesis 1–3 we find the beginning of this story, and it is there in the creation account that we see the divine design that God laid out within man. This design is the foundation for God's relationship with men and women throughout the whole of biblical history.

The Bible doesn't tell us every detail of the story. Genesis 1–3, in fact (and really up to Genesis 12), is as complete a telling of the story's beginning as God thought we needed in order for us to understand His design.

Many have viewed the creation account in Genesis through a scientific prism, from it finding insights into the grandeur with which God created. Others have viewed it through a historical prism, trying to decipher how long men and women have been here on Earth. Still others have viewed it through an astronomical prism, debating whether the six days of creation were twenty-four-hour days or something else. I, however, want to view this passage through a biographical prism, finding in it the essence of the whole story of the Bible—the story of God unilaterally acting to restore creation.

A Twofold Design: Relationship and Representation

In Genesis 1 God set the stage for the story: "In the beginning, God created" (Gen. 1:1). We find this creation process more fully explained by John in the opening words of his Gospel when he says of Jesus, "In the beginning was the Word, and . . . all things were made through him." So in the beginning there was heaven and earth; layered into the scene was light, then separation of light from darkness by day and night, then the separation of the waters, and then the creation of vegetation, fruit, and animals. Into each of the various types of plants and animals, God put the seed of multiplication. Finally upon this vast stage, immense to us but small to God, came man.

The words of the creation story call our attention to a specific detail regarding the shaping of man: "Then God said, 'Let us make man in our image, after our likeness'" (Gen. 1:26). Nothing else in God's creation is said to be made in the image and likeness of God Himself. God made mankind, male and female, in distinction to everything else in the universe—the stars, the earth, the vegetation, and the animal world.

People are like God in at least two ways. First, we are like Him in our ability to relate to other beings—to have relationship. This answers a question that every person from the very beginning of time has had, whether consciously or unconsciously: who am I? Ultimately, God designed us for relationship with Himself—to be loved by Him and to love Him in return. Who are we? We are His; we belong to Him.

The first man and woman, Adam and Eve, demonstrated this ability to have relationship with God. God related personally to Adam, walking with him in the cool of the evening in the garden, and we have no record that He related this way to any of the rest of His creation. Made in God's image and likeness, mankind can relate with God as well as with one another.

Of this first way in which man is like God, German theologian Erich Sauer, in his book *The Dawn of World Redemption*, says,

God, as the supreme lawgiver, has appointed the moral ordering of the world according to His nature, and He is love, the most perfect love (1 John 4:16). Therefore the moral appointment of free creatures must also be an appointment to love, and the supreme final purpose of world creation must consist in the self-unfolding and self-displaying of God as the Perfect, Holy, and Loving One, in the establishment of a fellowship of life and love between the Creator and the creature.[1]

Second, we are like God in that we can create and manage—and thus we are called to steward what God has given us, or represent Him in this world. Particularly, we are to represent God in the specific place where He puts each of us, managing the resources He gives us for His glory and living godly lives among the people around us. This answers a second question inherent in every man: why do I exist? We are created to represent God in this world—to participate with Him in His mission on this earth.

Adam represented God by stewarding the resources God had given him—the garden in which God had placed him and the animals that God had created and brought to him:

> *God said to them, "Be fruitful and multiply and fill the earth and subdue it, and have dominion over the fish of the sea and over the birds of the heavens and over every living thing that moves on the earth."... The Lord God took the man and put him in the garden of Eden to work it and keep it. (Gen. 1:28; 2:15)*

> *The Lord God had formed every beast of the field and every bird of the heavens and brought them to the man to see what he would call them. And whatever the man called every living creature, that was its name. The man gave names to all livestock and to the birds of the heavens and to every beast of the field. (Gen. 2:19–20)*

Representation of God in this world includes not only caring for the earth and handling our assets wisely but also living holy lives and loving our neighbor. This will look different for each of us as we fulfill our individual callings using our various gifts in the scattered places where we live.

Our representation of God in the earth, when we do it well, has impact beyond this world, as Sauer goes on to say:

> The extending of man's rule on the earth, provided he remained subject to God, signified a drawing of all things earthly into the sphere of the moral world-purposes, an increasing resumption of the earth for God and therewith a progressive leading forward of the creation to redemption and perfection. Paradise was thus the fixed point from which the uplifting of Nature into the sphere of the spirit should take its beginning. It was appointed by God to that purpose, "so that from here the whole earth should develop into a Paradise. The garden is the Holy of holies, Eden the holy place, the whole surrounding earth the vestibule and court. The climax is, that the whole shall be transformed into the glorified likeness of that Holiest."[2]

Demonstrating the inherent divine design of this twofold likeness to God, the Mosaic law reiterates the principle: "Hear, O Israel: The Lord our God, the Lord is one. You shall love the Lord your God with all your heart and with all your soul and with all your might" (Deut. 6:4–5). The law was meant to bring Israel into relationship with God, their Creator, protector, and sustainer. Then, once relationship with God was established, Israel was to represent Him to those around them: "You shall love your neighbor as yourself: I am the Lord" (Lev. 19:18).

Jesus said the same. When asked to give His estimation of the most important law given to Israel, He returned, I believe, not to these two passages in the Mosaic law but to the beginning of the human story—

to the way God created Adam and Eve in the first place. He responded with divine design:

> *You shall love the Lord your God with all your heart and with all your soul and with all your mind. This is the great and first commandment. And a second is like it: You shall love your neighbor as yourself. On these two commandments depend all the Law and the Prophets. (Matt. 22:37–40)*

While God does not answer every question we might have regarding our existence, He tells us enough in Genesis 1–3 to give us the dignity of being, relating, reproducing, and creating. We were created for relationship with God and representation of Him in the place He created for each of us. All expressions of human life flow from this essence and are defined and enriched by it.

Interdependency

A primary aspect of divine design, seen both in our relationship to God and our representation of Him to others, is interdependency. Created in God's image, we are to be like Him in our relationships with each other.

> In creation this interdependency was demonstrated in the working of the Trinity—Father, Son, and Holy Spirit: "God said, 'Let us make man in our image, after our likeness'" (Gen. 1:26). We see this divine design of the triune God acting in interdependency often throughout Scripture (see, for example, 2 Cor. 1:21–22; 13:14)—the same essence, same Being, yet made up of three different persons with different roles.[3]

This divine design of interdependency can be seen in other relationships brought about in the creation. For example, our planet is built upon just enough physical interdependencies between its various elements to allow Earth to sustain human life. Of this interdependency, Todd Woods of the Institute for Creation Research writes,

> If we apply the concept of "fellowship" to biology, we might expect the originally created organisms to have shown a stunningly high degree of interdependence. Because God desires His attributes to be perceived by all humans, this pattern would be expected to be prominent even after the Fall. A quick review of ecology indicates that this expectation is correct. It is possible to understand even some pathologies in this light. In a mutualistic relationship, two organisms live together and provide for the needs of the other.[4]

Interdependency, however, is perhaps most obviously reflected in marriage. When God created the stage of the universe, He placed Adam in His image and likeness in the garden of Eden to grow in his relationship to God and faithfully represent God in that place by stewarding all God had given him. Yet the Bible records that God saw Adam as incomplete:

> *The Lord God said, "It is not good that the man should be alone; I will make him a helper fit for him." Now out of the ground the Lord God had formed every beast of the field and every bird of the heavens. . . . But for Adam there was not found a helper fit for him. (Gen. 2:18–20)*

So, putting Adam into a deep sleep, God created Eve. He made her not out of something new or from something else in creation but out of Adam himself—out of a rib from his side. Upon awaking, Adam immediately recognized that Eve was like him—yet not fully like him. "Then the man said, 'This at last is bone of my bones and flesh of my flesh; she shall be called Woman, because she was taken out of Man'"

(Gen. 2:23). Men and women were, from the beginning, designed to be partners in all that God has designed for His human creation to accomplish in mission with Him.

Both the man and the woman are intended to seek relationship with God through His Word and through the indwelling Holy Spirit and in that daily seeking to respond to God in obedience. Their united lives become an incarnation of the effects of God's transforming grace in and through them, both individually and together. And the man and woman together are to represent God. God provides each of them with Spirit-given characteristics and gifts to use both independently and in a unified effort to steward the resources He gives them and reflect God to the world around them.

Divine Design Marred

When God created Adam and Eve, He created them in unconfirmed righteousness. That is, Adam and Eve were created righteous, but they were given the choice as to whether they would live in obedience to God, confirming their righteousness, or disobey God, leading to unrighteousness and separation from Him. We see their choice and their failure to obey vividly displayed in Genesis 3.

Because of Adam and Eve's disobedience and the subsequent passing on of a sinful nature to their progeny, God's divine design became distorted. For Adam, stewardship of the earth would become much more difficult: "Cursed is the ground because of you; in pain you shall eat of it all the days of your life; thorns and thistles it shall bring forth for you; and you shall eat the plants of the field. By the sweat of your face you shall eat bread" (Gen. 3:17–19). Eve's specific punishment particularly affected the marriage relationship: "Your desire shall be for your husband, and he shall rule over you" (Gen. 3:16). Because of her sin, she would suffer the tension of desire and willful resistance to Adam's authority.

In Adam and Eve's choice, the source and pervasive nature of rebellion resulting in sin was revealed. God did not author sin, but He allows it to exist and to appear at times to flourish within His ultimate designs.

The first sin was Satan's. Satan appeared on the scene in Genesis 3, having already been separated from his relationship with and representation of God (see Ezek. 28:11–19). He was an accuser, a liar, and a killer seeking only to take as many as possible with him in his rebellion. Jesus Himself revealed the nature of Satan: "He was a murderer from the beginning, and does not stand in the truth, because there is no truth in him. When he lies, he speaks out of his own character, for he is a liar and the father of lies" (John 8:44).

But the second sin was Adam and Eve's. The same kind of pride that drove Satan to rebel drove Adam and Eve to disobey God. Satan used the inherent struggle within them to entice the man and woman to reject God's provision and sustenance—to strike out on their own, under their own power, and in quest of their own destiny:

> *The serpent was more crafty than any other beast of the field that the Lord God had made. He said to the woman, "Did God actually say, 'You shall not eat of any tree in the garden'?" And the woman said to the serpent, "We may eat of the fruit of the trees in the garden, but God said, 'You shall not eat of the fruit of the tree that is in the midst of the garden, neither shall you touch it, lest you die.'" But the serpent said to the woman, "You will not surely die. For God knows that when you eat of it your eyes will be opened, and you will be like God, knowing good and evil." So when the woman saw that the tree was good for food, and that it was a delight to the eyes, and that the tree was to be desired to make one wise, she took of its fruit and ate, and she also gave some to her husband who was with her, and he ate.*
> *(Gen. 3:1–6)*

Adam and Eve did indeed discover a hidden quality to the fruit. More importantly, after eating it they discovered something new about themselves: they had lost the innocence that had come with their former willing obedience to God—His designs, provisions, and boundaries (see Gen. 3:7–8).

Separated from God's presence by their own choice, Adam and Eve were removed from the garden of God's presence and provision and made to walk in a world now hostile to God's intended designs. They would still relate to God but not as easily as they had in Eden. Ultimately, they would die, returning to the dust from which their bodies had been made: "By the sweat of your face you shall eat bread, till you return to the ground, for out of it you were taken; for you are dust, and to dust you shall return" (Gen. 3:19).

As long as they lived in their physical bodies, sin would be crouching at their door to bring them under its rebellious control. This painful reality would be passed on from them to their son Cain as well (see Gen. 4:3–7). From Cain and his siblings, this sinful nature would continue to the whole of Adam's race, resulting in the marring of God's divine design in all men and women throughout history.

Divine Design Restored

But Adam and Eve's moment of disobedience, an apparent victory for Satan, began the process of the ultimate victory mission that God now took upon Himself. Speaking to the devil, God pronounced both punishment and promise:

> *Because you have done this, you are cursed more than all cattle, and more than every beast of the field; on your belly you shall go, and you shall eat dust all the days of your life. And I will put enmity between you and the woman, and between your seed and her Seed; He shall bruise your head, and you shall bruise His heel. (Gen. 3:14–15, NKJV)*

The stage of history was now set. Because of this promise, God would birth the people through whom He would demonstrate His glory, justice, and salvation—the most important of whom would be His own Son, who would crush the head of the enemy—and He would establish them in their respective places. The original designs of God would not be thwarted but would be accomplished even more dramatically as God took upon Himself the re-creation of His people:

> *Sin came into the world through one man, and death through sin, and so death spread to all men because all sinned. . . . But the free gift is not like the trespass. For if many died through one man's trespass, much more have the grace of God and the free gift by the grace of that one man Jesus Christ abounded for many.*
> *(Rom. 5:12–15)*

God was not willing that we should be left to the mercy of our own sin. The heartbeat of human history, from the Bible's point of view, is the mercy of God resulting in the salvation of man. Blaise Pascal explained it this way:

> The world exists for the exercise of mercy and judgment, not as if men were placed in it out of the hands of God, but as hostile to God; and to them He grants by grace sufficient light, that they may return to Him, if they desire to seek and follow Him; and also that they may be punished, if they refuse to seek or follow Him.[5]

Because we continue to live in a fallen world, even for those of us who are redeemed by the life, death, and resurrection of Christ, the last Adam, "sin is crouching at the door" and desires to have us. Eventually, however, this restoration of the divine design will culminate in a final salvation out of this unrighteous world into a world of righteousness.

Living Out Divine Design

How then is this divine design to be carried forward in the lives of the children of God?

First and foremost, the authority of Scripture must be our first and only rule of faith, since it comes from and is actively preserved by a faithful and sovereign God. From the Bible we understand all that is necessary to live in this world. Genesis 1–12 contains all the words God thought we needed to be able to understand the origins of this universe and, more importantly, our own origins. Where this history deviates from the popular notions of the world we live in, the people of God must stand on the given revelation of God. Of course, we will continually grow in our understanding of those words, but we must reject ideologies clearly incompatible with the truth as revealed in Scripture and preserved by the Spirit of God over the ages of human history.

God created the world—that is the biblical given. How long it took, the ways in which He molded it into its final forms, and all the elements of its ongoing interdependence are open for discussion and discovery. The answers to these questions will ultimately demonstrate that they were created from His genius and are to be appreciated and understood within those boundaries. God also created Adam and Eve—there is no indication that they were evolved from other things that God created, including the animal world. He created mankind, both male and female, in His image, for the purpose of relationship and representation.

While God created all men and women in the image and likeness of the living God, because of the fall, all of us receive from Adam and Eve a corrupted nature, and thus the image of God in us is greatly marred. As a result, our relationship with God, our representation of God, and the interdependency between husband and wife, family members, and the whole of society are all affected!

The righteousness that God intended for us, however, can be restored in God's Son, Jesus Christ, who was born like man of a woman but remained like God in an uncorrupted nature. When we receive forgiveness of sins through Christ, we are counted as righteous by God, and we begin a relationship with God and a representation of Him that will continue for the duration of this life and into the new creation after time. "Rather was everything created with a purpose and a destiny; and our creation will be complete only when we have become what God designed."[6]

Our representation of God, birthed out of relationship with Him, is found in our service to Him. We are to exercise dominion over the world by stewarding it to the glory of God, and each of us does this by living out our individual calling. Additionally, as new creations in Jesus Christ, we are to represent to the world around us the mercy and grace of God offered in the gospel through our lives.

Os Guinness captures well this dual representation, or calling, that springs from relationship with God:

> Our primary calling as followers of Christ is by him, to him, and for him [relationship]. First and foremost we are called to Someone (God), not to something (such as motherhood, politics, or teaching) or to somewhere (such as the inner city or Outer Mongolia). Our secondary calling, considering who God is as sovereign, is that everyone, everywhere, and in everything should think, speak, live, and act entirely for him [representation]. We can therefore properly say as a matter of secondary calling that we are called to homemaking or to the practice of law or to art history. But these and other things are always the secondary, never the primary calling. They are "callings" rather than the "calling." They are our personal answer to God's address, our response to God's summons. Secondary callings matter, but only because the primary calling matters most.[7]

Marriage is a vital instrument of our representation of God in this world. Husbands and wives are brought together to fulfill the unique calling of God for them as a couple. This creates the framework for a godly family and a peaceable society.

God seeks men and women who understand His divine design and seek to live it out that others may come to know Him. Will we answer the call?

chapter 2

CREATED—AND RE-CREATED—IN THE IMAGE OF GOD

As we've discussed, Genesis 1 says that we are made in the image and likeness of God. What should we expect that to mean?

In John 8:25 the Pharisees, the Jewish religious leaders, asked a crucial question of Jesus: "Who are you?" Jesus' words surrounding that question reveal the historical and theological nature of the gospel: "You know neither me nor my Father. If you knew me, you would know my Father also" (John 8:19). Those who think they know God the Father without having placed their faith and trust in Jesus fail to recognize the divine nature and character of Jesus. It is only by embracing the truth about Jesus Christ that we are set free from sin and restored to divine design!

That truth, however, starts in the beginning.

Restored to God's Image—and Called to Perfection

What exactly was God's design when He created us in the image of God? We've already mentioned that we have the ability to have relationship with God and to represent God. But let's flesh this out further. What specifically makes men and women distinct and unique from the rest of God's creation?

We have cognition, that is, the ability to think. Animals reproducing a few impressive rudimentary skills in no way compares to the deductive and analytical ability given to mankind by our Creator. We have verbal skill, the ability to communicate what we are thinking, feeling, and anticipating. Of this skill Walter Kaiser, former president of Gordon-Conwell Theological Seminary, writes,

> Elsewhere we have attempted to develop another argument that would ground man's ability to communicate and to understand communication in the gift of the image of God. The general rules for interpreting do not appear to be formally learned, nor abstractly invented or discovered by man; rather they appear as part and parcel of his nature as an individual made in the image of God. The art of speaking and understanding has been in use from the moment God spoke to Adam in the Garden until now.[1]

We have relational skill, the ability to relate to others using our cognitive and verbal skills. We have the creative nature of God; we are able to invent—to take things, sometimes apparently unrelated things, and create something functional out of them. With our cognitive and creative skills, we have the ability to appreciate what we or others have created—to appreciate color, distinctions, surprises, and other things. Because we can communicate with, appreciate, and understand others, we can show concern, or have sympathy and empathy toward people. We can produce rational thought—we can think things through logically. We feel and therefore can show expression; in other words, we have and show emotion. We can think, relate, create, and therefore govern, or manage things and people.

But sin, as we know, impacted these likenesses of God in us. How deep, or to what extent, were these qualities affected by man's sinful choice?

Because of their sinful choice to disobey God, Adam and Eve's original righteous nature was displaced, resulting in a lawless human spirit and the marring of the image of God in mankind (see Rom. 5:12). Thus, the totality of mankind became corrupt, and human cognition, verbal skills, relationships, inventions, appreciations, deductions, concerns, emotions, rationalizations, and governing were no longer unadulterated. In fact, Paul tells us that "none is righteous, no, not one; no one understands; no one seeks for God. All have turned aside; together they have become worthless; no one does good, not even one" (Rom. 3:10–12).

C. S. Lewis paints a picture of the decay spread by man's sinful choice:

> "The story is not quite so simple as that," said the old woman, "so many things happened after the eating of the apple. For one thing, the taste created such a craving in the man and the woman that they thought they could never eat enough of it; and they were not content with all the wild apple trees, but planted more and more, and grafted mountain-apple on to every other kind of tree so that every fruit should have a dash of that taste in it. They succeeded so well that the whole vegetable system of the country is now infected: and there is hardly a fruit or a root in the land . . . that has not a little mountain apple in it. You have never tasted anything that was quite free from it."[2]

But all hope is not lost. Because of the promise made by God in Genesis 3:15 that His "Seed" would crush the enemy, Jesus came to Earth in the fullness of time and, by His death on the cross and His resurrection from the dead, crushed the head of the serpent. Because of His sacrifice for our sin and victory over death, we can be regenerated in the death, burial, and resurrection of Jesus and restored to the image God intended us to have when He first created man: "We were buried therefore with him [Jesus] by baptism into death, in order that, just as Christ was raised from the dead by the glory of the Father, we too might walk in newness of life" (Rom. 6:4–7). His seed is now planted in us, and we can now look and act like Jesus.

The remains of the flesh that we have from our likeness to sinful Adam are now to be dominated by our newly created likeness to Jesus:

> *Consider yourselves dead to sin and alive to God in Christ Jesus. Let not sin therefore reign in your mortal body, to make you obey its passions. Do not present your members to sin as instruments for unrighteousness, but present yourselves to God as those who have been brought from death to life, and your members to God as instruments for righteousness. (Rom. 6:11–13)*

Praise God! Although we are marred by sin, in Christ we are not bound by sin's power or demands. Instead we can live the life God intended for us when He created man in the garden.

The restored characteristics of the image of God found in a regenerate person are many. As believers in Christ, we now have an abounding appreciation toward all things. Paul says that we are to give thanks in all things and that in all circumstances he learned to abound (see Phil. 4:4–7, 10–13).

We have relational acceptance. Jesus says we are to pray for our enemies (see Matt. 5:43–48). Paul says that we should bear with one another (see Rom. 12:9–18). Jesus says that we should love our neighbor as ourselves (see Matt. 22:33–40), and Paul commands husbands to love their wives as their own bodies (see Eph. 5:25–28).

Released cognition enables us to see more clearly. Nebuchadnezzar, after he was greatly humbled by God, said twice that God's sovereignty extends over all things; imagine a king so high and mighty ultimately able to see his plight, recognize its significance, and come to this obvious cognitive conclusion (see Dan. 4). Paul wrote that nothing can separate us from the love of God; he had processed the things that God did in Jesus on our behalf and come to that conclusion (see Rom. 8). Jesus said that no one can take us from His hand—that if God cares for such small things as lilies and birds, won't He care (think about and provide) for us (see Matt. 6:25–30)?

Those who are re-created in Christ have renewed verbal skills. Paul says that we are to lay aside all coarse jesting (see Eph. 5:4) and rather to encourage one another with the resurrection and return of Jesus (see 1 Thess. 5:4–11). Jesus reminds us that every word we speak will be heard and judged (see Matt. 12:33–37).

We also have renewed concerns. Jesus says that peacemakers are like God their Father: "Blessed are the peacemakers, for they shall be called sons of God" (Matt. 5:9). And James tells us that pure and unde-filed religion is to care for the widow and orphan (see Jas. 1:26–27). The parable of the Good Samaritan reminds us that our neighbor's benefit is our concern (see Luke 10:25–37). Jesus also tells us that having been released from our Gentile life, we are to be like God, giving our lives in exchange for others:

> *The rulers of the Gentiles lord it over them, and their great ones exercise authority over them. It shall not be so among you. But whoever would be great among you must be your servant, and whoever would be first among you must be your slave, even as the Son of Man came not to be served but to serve, and to give his life as a ransom for many. (Matt. 20:25–28)*

In Christ we have renewed invention. Paul says that everything we do (an aspect of invention) is to be done to the glory of God, through the lens of serving God (see Eph. 6:5–9), and Jesus says that in our go-ing we are to make disciples (see Matt. 28:18–20).

All this restoration of God's image is possible for the renewed child of God because of the new people we have become in the death, buri-al, and resurrection of Jesus our Savior. We have been set free from the domination of sin: "For freedom Christ has set us free; stand firm therefore, and do not submit again to a yoke of slavery" (Gal. 5:1). Be-cause Christ's seed is now planted in us, we can be made by the Spirit into the people God our Father has intended us to become: "You therefore must be perfect, as your heavenly Father is perfect" (Matt. 5:48).

Restoration Is a Process

While the image of God has been restored in our lives, its practical impact is seen in our everyday lives in a progressive and maturing way. Even though we have been re-created in the image of God through the death, burial, and resurrection of Christ and sin no longer has dominion over us, the sinful nature we inherited from Adam still plagues us while we live in this fallen world. As long as we dwell in these bodies, we must constantly work against our sinful nature in order to grow consistently into the fullness of the image of Christ.

This is played out in our marriages, as husbands learn to love their wives as they love their own bodies and wives learn to love and respect their husbands; in our families, as fathers learn not to exasperate their children but to raise them in the fear of God and children learn to obey and honor their parents; in our neighborhoods, as we learn to love our neighbors as ourselves.

We see this increasing image of God in our church bodies, as people mature in the fruit of the Spirit and things like bitterness, gossip, and envy are flushed out of the life of the local body; we see it in our marketplaces, as Christians work as unto God in their daily callings and reflect His glory in their dealings with other people.

Our growth in the image of God is reflected in our decisions regarding our assets, as we learn to invest all we have in eternal things and to release our goods for the benefit of others. It is reflected in our ultimate expectations, as we mature in our understanding of the fact that we are sojourners in this world marred by sin, not residents of it. The progressive nature of the restored image of God in us is important for us to comprehend as we actively work and wait for the full restoration of the kingdom that God designed for His children from the beginning.

For the child of God, one day the remnants of our likeness to sinful Adam will be left behind upon our exit from this world into a new world that God will create free of sin:

> *If the tent that is our earthly home is destroyed, we have a building from God, a house not made with hands, eternal in the heavens. For in this tent we groan, longing to put on our heavenly dwelling . . . so that what is mortal may be swallowed up by life. He who has prepared us for this very thing is God, who has given us the Spirit as a guarantee. (2 Cor. 5:1–5)*

In that day our ability to steward the earth in full righteousness will be restored as well (see Rom. 8:19–21). But until that day, the process of the restoration of the image of God in us is of central importance as we "put on the new self, created after the likeness of God in true righteousness and holiness" (Eph. 4:24). This new self, confined to our sinful bodies, is capable of living unto God, and expected to do so, in both an old way and a new way (see Rom. 6)—old in the sense of how God created us to be before the fall and new in the sense that we have been restored to the image of God in Jesus Christ, the last Adam. The development of this new life is the essential focus of the Holy Spirit who now lives within us.

New Life Is Powerful

All the visible expressions of this new life described in the New Testament are predicated upon several things: the restored likeness and image of God in us (see John 3:1–8), the residency of the Holy Spirit in us to give us power (see Rom. 8:1–17), and our willing cooperation with Him (see Rom. 6). When we live the new life alongside unrestored people, our witness is powerful, because we demonstrate to them the image of God as He created it to be and as He intends it to be for those who will submit to the death, burial, and resurrection of Jesus Christ.

The story of God—His gospel—is about God acting to restore His creation back to Himself, and thus we cannot extract His purpose for creating man from this larger view. When we do, we run the risk of minimizing the full extent of God's work and purpose, and we short-circuit the miraculous work that God achieved in the death, burial, and resurrection of Jesus Christ. In other words, our presentation of this truncated gospel creates nominal Christians who appear to act on God's offer of salvation but fail to understand the transformative nature of the gospel message. Thus it produces "faith stillborns"—people who say that they belong to Jesus but never live or look like Him.

The only way for people to look like Jesus—to be re-created in the image of God—is to follow Christ into His death, burial, and resurrection so that man's original relationship to God and representation of God can be restored in their lives. Their old lawless man must be killed with Jesus on the cross and their new righteous self resurrected with Him in His resurrection. They are now re-created and able to live for God, in relationship with Him and representation of Him.

chapter 3

CULTIVATING RELATIONSHIP WITH GOD

With the image of God now restored to us, the way to relationship to God is once again open to us. This answers our deepest questions of identity, because who we are is rooted in being loved by God and loving Him in return. The psalmist's cry to God in Psalm 40 expresses a longing to enter into a deepening relationship with God our Father:

> *I waited patiently for the Lord; he inclined to me and heard my cry. He drew me up from the pit of destruction, out of the miry bog, and set my feet upon a rock, making my steps secure. He put a new song in my mouth, a song of praise to our God. Many will see and fear, and put their trust in the Lord. (Ps. 40:1–3)*

All too often, however, even for those of us who desire a deepening relationship with God, the world around us serves as an ever-increasing opiate. Perhaps the culture we live in is more sinful than past generations were, or maybe simply through the proliferation of media sin has become more present and accessible, but it seems to me that more and more Christians are experiencing relationship crises with God.

In 1742 Greek-language scholar John Bengel observed a reason for this problem:

Scripture is the foundation of the Church: the Church is the guardian of Scripture. When the Church is in strong health, the light of Scripture shines bright; when the Church is sick, Scripture is corroded by neglect; and thus it happens, that the outward form of Scripture and that of the Church, usually seem to exhibit simultaneously either health or else sickness; and as a rule the way in which Scripture is being treated is in exact correspondence with the condition of the Church.[1]

Some of those believers who fall into sin are nominal at best. They are perhaps the ones to whom Jesus refers in Matthew 7:23 when He says, "I never knew you; depart from me, you workers of lawlessness." They practice forms of Christianity but demonstrate none of the transformation or power promised by Jesus. The greatest danger of these people to the life of the church today is that they remain in and a part of it. Where once we may have seen them only in liberal churches, today they fill many evangelical churches.

Other Christians genuinely desire a deeper relationship with God, but they become preoccupied, drawn away by the opiate of the culture. Their reward is a growing sense of dryness toward the Scripture that they still hold to be true. For these believers a stark reappraisal of their lives and expectations is in order if they want to experience anything more than the forms of Christianity offered by the programs of too many churches.

To the rest of us, the call of the psalmist to enter into the mystery of redemption and abandon ourselves to God remains a promising invitation. When we remember moments with our heavenly Father, we recall in them warmth, encouragement, challenge, and yes, even correction. In those moments with God we knew that He was fully trustable and that to abandon ourselves to Him was no risk.

But even for those of us who deeply love God, there remains the constant need to preserve the time and discipline necessary to deepen our abandonment to Him. Deepening our relationship with God does not just happen—it must be worked on. I am not speaking of the legalism of Christian programs preached by too many churches but of the relational disciplines necessary to build upon the reconciliation given to us by the Father when we believed upon Jesus. Let's take a look at these disciplines.

Reconciliation Leading to Transformation

In 2 Corinthians 5:20 Paul reminds us, "We are ambassadors for Christ, God making his appeal through us. We implore you on behalf of Christ, be reconciled to God." This is where intimacy with God must begin: reconciliation to God through His Son. This is the first call of Scripture.

Reconciliation with God—restoration of the divine design—is the message of the Scriptures. It is inherent in Genesis 1–3. Man was born into relationship with God unlike any other being in God's creation; sin alienated us from God, but now in Jesus, the last Adam, the original purpose for which God created us can be restored.

This is the message of Jesus. In Matthew 22 and Mark 12 we see this clearly, where He tells us that the most important commandment in the Old Testament is to love the Lord God with all our hearts, souls, and minds. This is why Jesus came to Earth—that we might know the Father and the Son whom He sent. As believers we must make this our first order of business, or we are wasting people's time.

Beyond reconciliation, ongoing and deepening relationship to God is vital to our daily lives because we bring sin into our walk with God. Yes, all the judicial results of our sin were forever dealt with in the death, burial, and resurrection of Jesus; however, until we die and go to be with Him or He returns, the residue of our sinful selves, lingering in the members of our bodies, as Paul explains in Romans 6, wages battle against the depth of the relationship God planned for us when He made us.

That sin mars our daily lives as we daily do battle with jealousy, gossip, slander, and other sins. These qualities damage our relationships with other people, and the longer they hold any sway in our lives, the more scarring they produce in us. But God has a remedy for the scarring of today and the damage from the past.

We might wish that at the moment of salvation, all past damage was swept away and overcoming sin became the immediate norm. But such is not the case nor even the promise from God. As in any relationship, maintaining and strengthening our relationship to God demands discipline. I see at least four imperative disciplines advocated in Scripture that help strengthen our desire for deeper relationship with God.

Devotion to the Scriptures

The first discipline sets the stage for all the rest and is the foundation for the healing that God wants to bring to our lives: devotion to the Scriptures. The writer of Hebrews notes that God's Word is different from any other word:

> *The word of God is alive and active. Sharper than any double-edged sword, it penetrates even to dividing soul and spirit, joints and marrow; it judges the thoughts and attitudes of the heart. Nothing in all creation is hidden from God's sight. Everything is uncovered and laid bare before the eyes of him to whom we must give account. (Heb. 4:12–13, NIV)*

God's Word is alive, or God-breathed, and thus it can be continuously active in the lives of those who access it. The simple reading of the Word of God plants an active seed in the heart and mind of the reader, and that seed is meant to grow. In the unbeliever it can lead to conviction, repentance, and salvation. This can and does often happen, even with minimal input from anything or anyone else.

This same regenerative working continues for those of us who have already been reconciled with God and now need to build our relationship with Him. The consistent intake of God's Word by reading and studying plants seeds that release spiritual activity into our lives. The writer of Hebrews makes it clear that the cumulative effect of that activity is the exposé of our true selves. It enables us to see ourselves as sinful, flawed people; joint and marrow, soul and spirit are laid bare. God's Word leaves us no possibility of misunderstanding our broken condition—it leaves us naked before God and ourselves.

For too many this scenario evokes fear. To be so exposed to the piercing eye of God, to glimpse a clear picture of ourselves, is too much. So we hide! All too often we hide in superficially good things, perhaps in church programs or worship attendance. We are much more comfortable hearing someone else singing or preaching about relationship with God than we are with having it ourselves. Often our avoidance of Scripture is sheer laziness, but often it is simply fear—fear that no one is that trustable with such knowledge of us or even that we might not like what we see. But hiding only reinforces our pain, calcifies our scars, and worst of all, keeps us from transformation.

Nothing in this world is more capable of transforming us than God's Word. The exposition of our lives that comes from submitting to the reading of God's Word with a predisposed attitude of obedience always comes with the full clothing of our naked selves by Jesus, our high priest. Dressed in His clothes, we are exposed but not condemned. He has already taken all the condemnation for us.

In our reading of God's Word with a predisposed attitude to submit to it, then exposed for who we truly are but dressed in the full sufficiency of Jesus, we are invited into the presence of God Himself. In that presence we receive what we need: mercy to remind us of the forgiveness we already have in Jesus and grace as the transforming power of God is applied to our lives.

This transforming work, however, is a process, not a once-for-all revealing of our entire sinful selves. How could it be? If God exposed us at any one moment to all the scarring in our lives, could we handle it? We must build the amount of time we spend in God's Word as a consistent relational discipline. As a result, we will experience God's encouragement and joy as He exposes us for who we truly are, little by little, and shows us where we still need transformation.

Our relationship with God is a living thing. In reading God's Word we do not achieve a knowledge base that allows us to ignore further time spend with God in His Word; failing to nurture this most basic discipline is to regress in our relationship with God. Truth and knowledge of the Scriptures are vitally important in our relationship with God, but they will not replace the importance of the relationship itself. Moreover, truth alone will not protect the vitality that God offers us if it is not nurtured in intimate time with our heavenly Father.

I begin every day with the guidance of the Holy Spirit as He uses the Word of God that has been planted in my mind over time as well as any particular Scripture that I read that day to lead me into the places and relationships He wants. It is as if the pores of my spiritual life are cleansed each morning as I engage God in His Word. I am reminded of the things He holds most important—that I am on a journey sovereignly orchestrated by Him for His glory and the good of others and that the whole day is an opportunity for the restored and maturing righteousness of God to be demonstrated to others.

Silence

Silence is another necessary relational discipline. In Exodus 14:14 Moses reminded the children of Israel, "The Lord will fight for you; you need only to be still" (NIV). In Psalm 37:7 the psalmist reminds us, "Be still before the Lord and wait patiently for him; do not fret when people succeed in their ways" (NIV), and in Psalm 46:10, "Be still, and know that I am God."

In the noisy world in which we live, it often seems as if quiet places do not exist. But, in fact, silence is available to us on all sides. We just have to choose it. I have found that even in busy airports one can find silence, if one wants it. A person may have to walk a ways or sit in out-of-the-way places, but if silence is what he wants, he can find it.

Silence is a choice. It is choosing to turn off the noise of the world around us that is always clamoring for our attention. There are times and places for television, radio, social media, the next book, and people. But the depth of thinking and reflection that our souls desperately need begins to find space in our lives when we learn to choose and practice silence.

In silence we discover new joys. For example, the words we have planted into our hearts through the discipline of reading God's Word have the opportunity to flood our hearts and minds with new vigor and meaning. The beauty of the world that God made all around us speaks His power and sovereignty to us in silence. New confessions that God wants us to make can catch our attention. Above all, through silence, we become enthralled with God's presence.

I have not found a way to enter into the mystery of relationship with God without practicing the discipline of silence. We can find all kinds of reasons and excuses not to practice this discipline, but silence is a choice. Our lives will continue to be incomplete regarding God's design for our relationship with Him until we learn to practice regular periods of silence.

Solitude

If finding silence is difficult in our culture, finding solitude seems almost impossible. We find from the example of Jesus, however, that solitude must be pursued. Matthew 14:13 is one of a number of places in Scripture in which we find Jesus choosing to be alone: "He withdrew from there in a boat to a desolate place by himself." If Jesus sought out solitude, is it not necessary for us?

If we have been seduced into failing to forge times of listening to God in His Word, the problem may be that we really don't want to be alone with ourselves. Is fear of self-discovery one of the things that keep us from desiring solitude? Our culture reigns king in keeping us busy enough to guarantee that we will not have time to be alone and quiet, but our culture is nothing more than smoke and mirrors, a mere disturbance and distraction from the disciplines of silence and solitude.

In solitude there is space for silence as well as for actively listening to God in His Word. In solitude we are reminded of the brevity and temporariness of our lives on this planet. More importantly, we are reminded that we were not created for this world, which is dominated by the effects of sin. The world God created for us in Genesis 1 is the one we were created for, and it is the one to which we will be restored.

Solitude provides much-needed moments of resetting the compass of our lives. But above all, in solitude we discover that we are not really alone. God is there.

Submission

A final relational discipline that is both necessary and enriching in our relationship to God is submission. The writer of Hebrews reminds us,

> *We have all had human fathers who disciplined us and we respected them for it. How much more should we submit to the Father of spirits and live! (Heb. 12:9, NIV)*

> *During the days of Jesus' life on earth, he offered up prayers and petitions with fervent cries and tears to the one who could save him from death, and he was heard because of his reverent submission. Son though he was, he learned obedience from what he suffered. (Heb. 5:7–8, NIV)*

"Submission" is a word charged with misunderstanding and fear. Paul's own words that he was a "slave of Christ Jesus" (Rom. 1:1, HCSB) have been equally misunderstood. If God is the sovereign Creator of this planet as Genesis asserts; if God has fearfully and wonderfully made us even while we were in our mother's womb, as the psalmist asserts (see Ps. 139:13–14); and furthermore, if the Creator has a right to expect that the creation will respond to His loving wisdom, then how could we not expect wholehearted and willing submission to Him to be a natural outflow of our relationship to Him?

Both Paul and Jesus understood the true nature of submission. Their submission was couched in the reality of relationship with and trust in the One whom they know intimately.

God invites us to trust Him. Practicing the disciplines of Scripture, silence, and solitude increases our trust in Him, and this helps submission to become our default response in our relationship to God. This ought to be our goal.

Our conviction about the truth and thus reliability of what God has revealed in His Word demands and provokes a predisposition to obedience to Him in our minds. Learning to hear Him in His Word, in silence, and in aloneness works to increase the obedient, submissive response He wants in our heart and life decisions.

The world around us and the flesh within us, both agitated by Satan and the enemies of God, conspire to keep us from relationship with the heavenly Father. But across thousands of years, many have been willing to take the risk of relationship with God, and it has been evidenced in them by lives of devotion to the Scriptures, silence, solitude, and submission. The invitation remains—let us abandon ourselves to God!

chapter 4

REPRESENTING GOD IN THE WORLD

Out of the ongoing richness of our relationship with Him, God has made us to represent Him.

In the beginning God created Adam and Eve, unlike anything else in His creation, to be in relationship with Him. Jesus described this relationship as loving the Lord our God with all our hearts, souls, and minds. This is the very nature of the human life as God designed it in the beginning. As such, relationship with the Lord is the first call that God puts on our lives. But out of this call to relationship comes the call to service, or representation of God. Os Guinness aptly defines this secondary call:

> Calling is the truth that God calls us to himself so decisively that everything we are, everything we do, and everything we have is invested with a special devotion and dynamism lived out as a response to his summons and service.[1]

This call to represent God to the world around us is in actuality an invitation from Him to share in His mission to restore creation to Himself. Our representation of God is expressed in multiple ways, but we live it out primarily in our stewardship of God's creation and through our increasing holiness as we grow in relationship to God. Both means are a reflection of God's image and likeness to the world around us.

Representing God by Stewarding His Creation

In the beginning Adam represented God by caring for the garden God had created for him to live in and naming the animals. Adam and Eve were given dominion over all creation. They were to exercise authority—not an authority inherent in them but the authority of God who had called them to represent Him in and among His creation.

As with relationship, this divine design to represent God requires men and women to embrace it and respond to it, but Adam and Eve's failure to do this marred God's original intention for representation. They crossed God's boundaries in exercising His authority over creation, instead choosing their own desires and thus marring the image of God in men and women and corrupting God's call on our lives. Rather than faithfully representing God by subduing and multiplying the earth according to His design, Adam and Eve selfishly sought to be like God in ways that He had not designed or granted. They believed the lie of Satan that the wisdom they would gain in eating the fruit would give them equality with God.

So God's image in them and therefore their callings were marred—but they were not destroyed. God limited the lifespan of man so that He could ultimately fully restore His image and thus His calling in those He would one day redeem through His Son, the last Adam—the God-man, Jesus Christ. Bible scholar F. F. Bruce explains this restoration of representation: "God has put everything under the dominion of human beings, and it was the nature of humans—our nature—that the Son of God took upon himself in order to win back this dominion."[2]

Every man and woman, whether a believer or not, still bears the image and likeness of the One who created them. Unbelievers are limited by sin and disobedience, and they distort the calling and mission God designed for them, being consumers of life rather than those who live for God's kingdom and glory. Those who do not know Christ have suffered the lie of Satan that there is something greater, safer, and more fulfilling that what God originally promised.

But even those of us who are redeemed and restored through God's Son do not fully live out the purpose of God for our lives. God's image is maturing progressively in our lives as we learn to submit to the Father's will and give the indwelling Holy Spirit the right to mature us into the image of the Son, Jesus Christ, and as we consistently listen to God through His Scriptures—the Bible.

We see the marring of man's authority over God's creation in the Lord's dealings with the people of Noah's day. God pronounced judgment upon the animals and people of the earth, but He left the earth intact to be repopulated by Noah and his family:

All flesh died that moved on the earth, birds, livestock, beasts, all swarming creatures that swarm on the earth, and all mankind. Everything on the dry land in whose nostrils was the breath of life died. He blotted out every living thing that was on the face of the ground, man and animals and creeping things and birds of the heavens. They were blotted out from the earth. Only Noah was left, and those who were with him in the ark. (Gen. 7:21–23)

We also see it in the many "care for the earth" admonitions that God gave His people in Israel. The land was even to be given a complete rest every seven years (see Lev. 25:1–7). Surely Israel would have questioned whether leaving a field alone for a whole year was a wise economic decision, but God the Creator knew that a year of rest would make the land more fertile in the future. Further, every fifty years God further mandated a more complete restitution for His creation. Israel was to take a year not only to rest but to reset the corruption that had accumulated over the previous half century by declaring a year of jubilee and liberty (see Lev. 25:8–17).

Not only was our representation of God marred by the disobedience of Adam and Eve, but God's design in the earth itself was marred. The present earth labors under this marring and indeed longs for the day of restoration:

> The creation waits with eager longing for the revealing of the sons of God. For the creation was subjected to futility, not willingly, but because of him who subjected it, in hope that the creation itself will be set free from its bondage to corruption and obtain the freedom of the glory of the children of God. For we know that the whole creation has been groaning together in the pains of childbirth until now. (Rom. 8:19–22)

One day, however, this proclivity to death will be fully reversed at the return of Jesus Christ, when God will also usher in a new heaven and a new earth.

Representing God by Reflecting His Character

Dominion over the creation is not the only aspect of representation that God designed for the children of Adam and Eve. We are also created to represent Him by reflecting His character in and to the world. Another way to say this might be that we are to love our neighbor. God, through Moses, gave a clear picture of this to Israel:

> When you reap the harvest of your land, you shall not reap your field right up to its edge, neither shall you gather the gleanings after your harvest. And you shall not strip your vineyard bare, neither shall you gather the fallen grapes of your vineyard. You shall leave them for the poor and for the sojourner: I am the Lord your God.
>
> You shall not steal; you shall not deal falsely; you shall not lie to one another. You shall not swear by my name falsely, and so pro-

fane the name of your God: I am the Lord.

You shall not oppress your neighbor or rob him. The wages of a hired worker shall not remain with you all night until the morning. You shall not curse the deaf or put a stumbling block before the blind, but you shall fear your God: I am the Lord.

You shall do no injustice in court. You shall not be partial to the poor or defer to the great, but in righteousness shall you judge your neighbor. You shall not go around as a slanderer among your people, and you shall not stand up against the life of your neighbor: I am the Lord.

You shall not hate your brother in your heart, but you shall reason frankly with your neighbor, lest you incur sin because of him. You shall not take vengeance or bear a grudge against the sons of your own people, but you shall love your neighbor as yourself: I am the Lord. (Lev. 19:9–18)

God is holy, and His people, brought into being by His gracious acts and preservation, are to be like Him. He says through Moses, "You shall be holy to me, for I the Lord am holy and have separated you from the peoples, that you should be mine" (Lev. 20:26). Israel's representation of God would be a blessing to the nations, who would see Him and His designs in God's people. As a result, the nations would be drawn to God and blessed by Him. As God said to Abraham, "In your offspring shall all the nations of the earth be blessed, because you have obeyed my voice" (Gen. 22:18).

God's glory was also to be seen in His people's obedient following of the law. His words were life and were to be "eaten" that Israel in turn might have life. The nations, seeing this life, would be drawn to God and would come to understand how He had chosen, preserved, and given life to His people that others too might give Him glory. The psalmist wrote of Israel,

> *May God be gracious to us and bless us and make his face to shine upon us, that your way may be known on earth, your saving power among all nations. Let the peoples praise you, O God; let all the peoples praise you! Let the nations be glad and sing for joy, for you judge the peoples with equity and guide the nations upon earth. (Ps. 67:1–4)*

So it is for the people of God today who have been called out of every tribe, tongue, and nation. We too are to show the glory and holiness of our Father who is holy. Peter clearly says, "As obedient children, do not be conformed to the passions of your former ignorance, but as he who called you is holy, you also be holy in all your conduct, since it is written, 'You shall be holy, for I am holy'" (1 Pet. 1:14–16).

Because of the death, burial, and resurrection of Jesus Christ and the indwelling presence of God through the Holy Spirit in our bodies, we are capable of denying the passions of the flesh that war against our new nature created after the likeness of Jesus Christ in righteousness and of living lives that begin to undo the marring of sin in mankind. We have a growing capacity to faithfully steward the assets that God puts into our hands and to represent Him in this world through righteous life choices.

Our lives are to increasingly become a reflection of our Father, whose "Seed" has been planted in us (see Gen. 3:15) so that we can be like Him as He has revealed Himself through His Son, Jesus Christ. As we saw in chapter 2 of this book, this makes God's standard for us a high one: "You therefore must be perfect, as your heavenly Father is perfect" (Matt. 5:48). Jesus makes this truth clear in the Sermon on the Mount, which we will examine later. I like to think of Jesus' words not so much as a challenge but as a promise. We have been redesigned by God, through Jesus, to be like Him, just as He designed Adam and Eve in the beginning, and now we bear the seed of our heavenly Father.

John says, "No one born of God makes a practice of sinning, for God's seed abides in him, and he cannot keep on sinning because he has been born of God" (1 John 3:9).

God's life beats within our new nature, and we are able to obey His designs through the disciplines and decisions in our lives. As we regularly engage Him in His Word, the Holy Spirit gives us words of reminder and maturation. He calls us to choose His revealed definitions of life in this world, revelations that demonstrate His glory and designs for His creation. We must consistently choose His revelations and reject the ever-present urges of the flesh still operating in the members of our bodies. Though our bodies are dead because of sin, our spirits are alive with Jesus Christ. As we give our bodies to the Spirit who lives within us, we become instruments of the righteousness of God that He wants to express in and through us and can consider ourselves "dead to sin and alive to God in Christ Jesus" (Rom. 6:11).

Despite the rebellion initiated by Adam and Eve, God intends to fulfill His creative design for the earth and for us. In Christ this design finds as much expression and extension as it will until God destroys this world in favor of a new world of righteousness.

Maturing Progressively in the Life of Christ

Those of us who are followers of Jesus Christ mature by obeying the Spirit who is within us and defying the flesh that continues in the members of our bodies. But what stops our indulgence of the flesh so that the life of Christ, placed in us through the new birth, can be formed in us? Remember what God said to Cain: "Sin is crouching at the door. Its desire is for you, but you must rule over it" (Gen. 4:7). In Colossians 2–3 Paul outlines how we can rebuff the work of the flesh and embrace the daily victory available to us so that we can faithfully represent Christ in this world.

To have died with Christ is to have been delivered from the dictates of the flesh and the regulations that go with a false kind of religion.

These false regulations have no power to control the urges of the flesh. They make us feel better about ourselves in a false and superficial way, but they are powerless against the flesh (see Col. 2:20–23). But in Christ we can put off the flesh in regard to its dominion over us:

> *In him the whole fullness of deity dwells bodily, and you have been filled in him, who is the head of all rule and authority. In him also you were circumcised with a circumcision made without hands, by putting off the body of the flesh, by the circumcision of Christ. (Col. 2:9–11)*

Christ has done what was necessary to restore the original designs of God, restore us to the Father, and give us relationship with Him once again. This once-for-all action gives birth to a daily implication: we can learn to say no to the desires of the flesh and yes to the new life of God in us.

If we have been raised with Christ, it only follows naturally that our lives should display that truth. We must seek the things above, because that is where Christ is now seated. We must allow our minds to be filled with the things in heaven and not dominated by the things on Earth, for when this life is over, it is that place and that life that we will inherit (see Col. 3:1–4).

Because of this new life with Christ, we need to daily put to death the life we inherited from Adam and Eve. That life is earthly and will cease to exist when we die. It is dominated by everything that is antagonistic to the righteousness that God designed for us in the beginning. Our new life is restored in Jesus Christ and will be our full position in eternity:

> *Put to death therefore what is earthly in you: sexual immorality, impurity, passion, evil desire, and covetousness, which is idolatry. On account of these the wrath of God is coming. In these you too once walked, when you were living in them. But now you must*

put them all away: anger, wrath, malice, slander, and obscene talk from your mouth. Do not lie to one another, seeing that you have put off the old self with its practices and have put on the new self, which is being renewed in knowledge after the image of its creator. Here there is not Greek and Jew, circumcised and uncircumcised, barbarian, Scythian, slave, free; but Christ is all, and in all. (Col. 3:5–11)

We are to put on and act out the new life of Jesus alive in us due to His death on our behalf and the presence and power of the Holy Spirit in us. Rather than being self-serving, those of us who are in Christ, like God, are to be focused on serving others. Because we bear the image of God and can see beyond this life, we must embrace relationship to others with compassion, kindness, humility, and other godly traits:

Put on then, as God's chosen ones, holy and beloved, compassionate hearts, kindness, humility, meekness, and patience, bearing with one another and, if one has a complaint against another, forgiving each other; as the Lord has forgiven you, so you also must forgive. (Col. 3:12–13)

Above all this, because of the love that God has demonstrated toward us, the new nature that He has given us, and the indwelling of the Spirit, we are to allow love for our brother and sister to dominate our responses. When we face conflict, our minds and hearts should be full of God's words so that we can let the peace of Christ rule in us: "Put on love, which binds everything together in perfect harmony. And let the peace of Christ rule in your hearts, to which indeed you were called in one body" (Col. 3:14–15).

When we put on Christ, we become the representation of God—His nature, His designs, and His ends. As we live in Him, we are able to steward His creation and live out His holiness and love to the people around us. What a privilege to be called to share in the mission of God in this world!

chapter 5

HEIRS TOGETHER OF THE GRACIOUS GIFT OF LIFE

Divine design, as we have clearly seen, consists in relationship with God and representation of Him in this world. But a vital aspect of that design and its outworking consists in man's interdependency. While interdependency is essential to every relationship, beginning with the Trinity and reflected in every aspect of family and society, nowhere is it seen more obviously as in marriage.

The words of the apostle Peter about husbands and wives being "heirs together of the grace of life" (1 Pet. 3:7, NKJV) caught my attention many years ago. This idea is so radically different from what we observe in the world around us, in which a growing hostility has developed between men and women and carried into the marriage relationship. This hostility has been unleashed in the church as well.

Not only is this contrary to God's design, it runs the risk of imploding all human relationships in marriage, in family, and in the marketplace. I can understand a heightened degree of protest when women suffer overt abuse and slavery. But while Christians ought to be bold in decrying abusive treatment of women, we are not to partner in the attitudes that create it.

The world's antagonism toward the divine design and the new aggressive forms of protest this antagonism creates also usher in a societal confusion regarding gender. But anything outside the clear and appealing design of God for men and women is convoluted with questions that begin with people rather than God. Start with anything other than God's design, and we walk in disobedience and therefore confusion.

Against the backdrop of this confusion, these words of Peter hold an appealing promise: my wife, Patti, and I can be heirs together of the gracious gift of life. These words call to me. Heirs together! My wife and I are not meant to be in antagonism toward each other but to share life together. We are heirs, both of us, of the promise made by God to Adam and Eve and their posterity that runs from Genesis to Revelation: "I will put enmity between you and the woman, and between your seed and her Seed; He shall bruise your head, and you shall bruise His heel" (Gen. 3:15, NKJV). The church now lives and declares that promise, waiting for the full restoration that God has planned, and Patti and I share in it together.

This promise is life eternal, but it is also life here on Earth together—a harmonious shared life that only God could have conceived of enjoying His creation, building a family, and taking pleasure in companionship. For as long as we live, Patti and I can anticipate together God's promise of eternal life and serve Him together in this life. As we do, we will work, enjoy God's creation, and build a family of children and grandchildren who for generations to come will see our model of togetherness and be drawn to God. In that word "together" is wrapped up all the potential grandeur that two people this side of eternity can find. At its core we find a journey that requires faith and provides fellowship, friendship, intimacy, and the fruit of family.

In these thoughts on the togetherness of God's creation for man and woman, I will not delve into issues about communication or interpersonal understanding, mainly because the hostility that often rises between married men and women, and among men and women in general, rises from our flesh (read rebellion against divine design). We want what we want. If that attitude is not crucified, it will create all the havoc implied by God's pronouncements on Adam, Eve, and the serpent in Genesis 3.

Many books have been written on the topic of marriage, and while many of them are good, an equal number of them are useless, primarily because they start with man and woman and not with God. If God made us, let's start with Him, His Word, and His design.

Man and Woman in God's Image and Likeness

In the beginning God created them male and female. Both Adam and Eve were distinct from everything He had created before them—for they alone were made in God's image and likeness, each of them for relationship with God and representation of Him. They were also created to be interdependent, just as the God who had created them—Father, Son, and Holy Spirit—and the world they lived in were. With some reflection a lesson becomes clear: if we extract the role of interdependency in marriage, family, or society, then damage, often irreparable, is done to all parts.

Men and women represent God in ways similar to each other but also in unique ways. Adam and Eve were equally made in God's image—Adam by God's direct creation of him out of the dust of the earth and Eve by God's creation of her out of Adam. However, they were not two Adams or two Eves. On the basis of His image and likeness, God created uniqueness specific to a man and specific to a woman.

Adam immediately recognized sameness yet diversity when he saw Eve for the first time. He said of her, "This at last is bone of my bones and flesh of my flesh; she shall be called Woman, because she was taken out of Man" (Gen. 2:23). Genesis 3:20 goes on to tell us, "The man called his wife's name Eve, because she was the mother of all living." Adam was not created to be a mother and so acknowledged Eve's differentness from him.

While both man and woman were created in God's image, God Himself is neither male nor female, for He is not man—He is God. But the diverse way in which males and females are created represents a more complete picture of the character of God than either of them alone can.

The Fall and Its Consequences in Men and Women

Into the idyllic context of the garden of Eden, Satan introduced sin. Adam and Eve embraced his lies and thereby introduced "flesh" as the operating system to all their offspring. Everything in the universe was marred from its original design and purpose, including the image of God in men and women.

The situation at the fall of Adam and Eve from God into sin was much more serious and dangerous than Christians often realize. The disobedience of Adam and Eve not only introduced the flesh as man and woman's operating system, it brought with it resulting curses. These consequences sit over every generation of men and women everywhere on the earth.

It began with Adam struggling to bring forth food from the earth, as the garden of divinely designed multiplication was now closed off to him. Outside the garden Adam toiled to gain food from the plants, trees, and animals, but they were no longer easily managed under his hand. Future generations worked against this inherent restriction. Their means of labor changed from agriculture to machines to technology, but their daily struggles to succeed continued. Not only did they work long and hard, but unscrupulous people continually worked to bring the primary benefit to themselves, even at the cost of others.

Flesh corrupted people's interpersonal relationships as well. Eve struggled to accept that Adam, as the firstborn, stood first in God's stewardship authority over the earth. Without the flesh Adam and Eve would have lived out this order in harmony like that of the Trinity. But they chose "freedom" and harvested a propensity to unilateralism and independence. The fruit of this for Eve was a desire for her counterpart, Adam, but also the repelling of dependency on him. The relationship between the two was meant by God to be centered upon their need of each other, but Adam and Eve chose the self-centeredness of the flesh over the harmony of interdependency.

Give in to these fleshly desires and actions long enough, and all God-given gender uniqueness, along with the design of interdependency, is lost. Hostility and competition replace the divine design. The result is confusion in gender, broken marriages, destroyed families, and even imploding societies.

Men and women, even those who are unredeemed, cannot ignore the divine design without suffering the consequences. Some do learn to dominate the more obvious expressions of the flesh and thereby experience the fruit of divine design in part. But when culture begins to break down and the willfulness of the corrupt heart takes center stage, the already corrupted genius of God in men and women will eat away at the God-planned experience of joy until the connections between men and women are strained to the breaking point.

When this occurs, all the God-ordained categories established in creation are turned upside down. An ever-increasing public display of disobedience becomes the championed norm, the consequences of sin in Genesis 3 tear apart human bonds, and any kind of corruption from the minds of men and women becomes possible. Societies that reach this point are on a death march.

Good News for the Marriage Relationship

Flesh has damaged the image and likeness of God in men and women. But the good news is that it can be restored in Jesus Christ. Not perfectly—perfection awaits Christ's return, when this body and its flesh will be left behind. But for those of us in Christ, the Holy Spirit indwelling our newborn lives will rebuild God's original intentions in our personal awareness and in our marital unions.

Through the Word of God and the Holy Spirit within us, we can understand God's original design and begin to embrace and act on it. We can learn to say no to the flesh, because the Holy Spirit will give us the power to do so. But we will need to do so on God's already revealed designs and purposes. Anything less allows the flesh to once again introduce actions contrary to God's designs, which will result in pain, undone marriages, destroyed families, split churches, and, ultimately, defamation of the name and glory of God to a watching world. We cannot take God's design too seriously any more than we can diminish our ongoing battle with the flesh and its consequences.

If we are to understand and grow in our marriage relationships, we must begin where the Bible begins: the creative genius of God. God designed marriage with regard, care, and provision for the need of the men and women He created. He understands both men and women, for He made them. God created men and women to be partners, and while the fall mars their ability to carry out this design, it does not negate the design.

Principles for Interdependent Marriage

So what does a godly marriage look like? What does God tell us in His Word about this design for man and woman that He ordained?

First, the husband and wife are to be partners in their relationship to God and in their representation of Him. To pursue relationship with God, both the man and woman must seek God through His Word and through the indwelling Holy Spirit, and in that daily seeking each must respond to God in obedience. God intends to be the first focus of each life. This core relationship with God in both the man and woman prepares each of them for greater meaning and unity in their marriage and faithfulness in their family.

Equally, the man and woman are to represent God. To enable them to do this, God provides each of them with Spirit-given gifts as well as godly characteristics (fruit of the Spirit). At times they use these gifts and characteristics independently, although in mutual agreement as to where, how, and when they should be used; at other times they use them in a unified effort. Either way, God intends to display Himself to others through these gifts and characteristics.

When it comes to the gifts of the Spirit, the man and woman must understand and embrace the words of God given through Paul in 1 Corinthians 12:7: "To each is given the manifestation of the Spirit for the common good." They are to help each other understand their respective gifts and release them to serve others.

Regarding the fruit of the Spirit, their service to others is often the result of time spent with God in His Word and His Spirit working in them. They show compassion, extend hospitality, share their assets, and minister encouragement as they represent God to the people around them. Galatians 5:22–23 details this fruit: "The fruit of the Spirit is love, joy, peace, patience, kindness, goodness, faithfulness, gentleness, self-control; against such things there is no law."

First and foremost this fruit is poured out into the marital relationship as both the man and woman learn a new level of respect, honor, appreciation, and service toward each other, but it is poured out into other relationships as well. Being incrementally formed into the image of Christ, the man and woman love those whom the world deems unlovable. They open their hearts, wallets, and homes to the unprotected and care tangibly for those in need. The psalmist declares the heart of God in this matter: "Father of the fatherless and protector of widows is God in his holy habitation" (Ps. 68:4–5).

In summary, the husband and wife become the incarnation of the words of Jesus in Matthew 5: they are the poor in spirit, those who mourn, the meek, those who hunger and thirst for righteousness, the merciful, the pure in heart, and the peacemakers. Thus they shall be called sons and daughters of God. As each matures in their relationship with God and brings that maturity into their marriage relationship, the husband and wife catch the joy of representing God with all that they have and are. They turn the world's expectations of marriage upside down.

Second, in God's design for marriage, the man and woman become one. This is a mystery. The most obvious proof of this oneness is children, who are a unique blend of the DNA patterns of mother and father. But over time, as they intensify in the spiritual disciplines of spending time with God in His Word and listening to the Holy Spirit, the husband and wife become one in more than offspring.

They grow in oneness by learning to increasingly love each other. The first place the growing new fruit of the Spirit will be most felt is in the marriage relationship. As they become one, the husband and wife will learn to treat each other with love, joy, peace, long-suffering, gentleness, and other godly fruit. Of course healthy communication patterns help, and good listening goes a long way, but it is the Holy Spirit who makes transformed human relationships most possible.

They also learn to share in wisely handling the assets that God places in their hands to steward for Him. Is there any more inflammatory issue in marriage than how to handle money? Yet over time disagreements on this issue can fade into the background as the couple learns to submit to God's ownership of their assets. They can then pursue a unified approach to stewarding their assets to God's glory and the expansion of His kingdom.

Husbands and wives also become unified in the influence they have on their children. As the man and woman submit to God's designs and purposes for their family, God helps them faithfully manage their home. Oneness is powerful, which is exactly why God designed it from the very beginning: "A man shall leave his father and his mother and hold fast to his wife, and they shall become one flesh" (Gen. 2:24).

Third, in marriage the husband and wife are brought together by God. It is God who joins husband and wife together; marriage is His created design. Because of this, man is mandated to bless and respect the union. In Matthew 19:6 Jesus reiterates and expands this idea: "They are no longer two but one flesh. What therefore God has joined together, let not man separate."

Marriage is not a divine afterthought; it is a centerpiece to the divine design that God intended when He made male and female. Subverting this design brings with it natural consequences. Ripping apart that which God has woven into one from two brings pain to both parts and all the other parts connected to it. God stands against divorce as a rejection of His provision and therefore a rejection of Him.

Fourth, in a godly marriage the husband and wife are co-heirs of life. God did not create Adam and Eve to live in antagonism toward each other; He created them for life and intended them to live that life together. The fall has made that more difficult, but it is not impossible. The second Adam restored the life that God designed us to have, at least in as full an expression as is possible this side of eternity.

Just think for a minute of all the good things that come to mind with the word "life"—sunrises, sunsets, walks, leisure time, activities to serve others, children, grandchildren. All these have been designed by God for the husband and wife to enjoy together. But in some way these things will be extended and appreciated in eternity, as Randy Alcorn points out in his book *Heaven*:

> Receiving a glorified body and relocating to the New Earth doesn't erase history, it culminates history. Nothing will negate or minimize the fact that we were members of families on the old Earth. My daughters will always be my daughters, although first and foremost they are and will be God's daughters. My grandchildren will always be my grandchildren. Resurrection bodies presumably have chromosomes and DNA, with a signature that forever testifies to our genetic connection with family.[1]

Fifth, God will judge those who do not respect the marriage vow. Malachi 2 teaches us of the seriousness with which God treats the marriage union and the judgments that come to those who break it by divorce:

> *The Lord was witness between you and the wife of your youth, to whom you have been faithless, though she is your companion and your wife by covenant. Did he not make them one, with a*

portion of the Spirit in their union? And what was the one God seeking? Godly offspring. So guard yourselves in your spirit, and let none of you be faithless to the wife of your youth. "For the man who does not love his wife but divorces her, says the Lord, the God of Israel, covers his garment with violence, says the Lord of hosts. So guard yourselves in your spirit, and do not be faithless."
(Mal. 2:14–16)

Since God is the Creator of both men and women and the inventor of marriage, we ought not to be surprised that He also pronounces a judgment upon those who disregard Him. That disregard of His design regarding the permanency of marriage has two damning consequences.

One, because divorce is a rejection of God's sovereignty, God sets Himself against those who carry it out. The marriage story begins in Genesis, and when we reject God's place for us in creation and choose our own way, God "no longer regards [our] offering or accepts it with favor from [our] hand" (Mal. 2:13). God observes the covenant we make with our spouses and regards unfaithfulness of any kind as a disregard of that covenant and the importance He places on it.

And two, because divorce is a rejection of God's goodness in creating things in His way, God rejects the religious actions of those who choose it. Again, the story begins in Genesis: "It is not good that the man should be alone" (Gen. 2:18). When we disregard this provision by God of the deep need of men and, by extension, of women, God is displeased. The very nature of the marriage union defines its permanence here on Earth—the man and woman become one. This permanence is not to be rejected by us or subverted by others.

Sixth, marriage must be protected. Because we still battle with the flesh, we must do all we can to protect marriage. We protect it in our hearts, giving it first priority after our relationship with God. We protect it with our wills, giving it time and nurturing the disciplines necessary to grow it. We give it priority in our minds, taking time to ponder and meditate on it.

Marriage must also be protected because its divine design results in intimacy like no other relationship on Earth. The writer of Hebrews adds to the serious words of Malachi when he says that "marriage should be honored by all, and the marriage bed kept pure, for God will judge the adulterer and all the sexually immoral" (Heb. 13:4, NIV).

Without a doubt, once adultery or sexual immorality is committed by a person, the spiritual disciplines of being in the Word, using spiritual gifts, growing in love for each other, and giving of assets together have clearly not been practiced for a long time, if ever. But as the writer of Hebrews promises, God will judge those who fail to protect their marriages. He may do it by the sociological implosion of family in society or even health-related issues, but whatever the means of God's judgment, we ought not to be surprised at anything that exists below the surface in people or cultures that reject God's designs and live in opposition to it.

What ought to surprise us is when confessing Christians, especially leaders, fall into such patterns. Of course this is possible because the flesh still inhabits the body, and there is, as we know, a remedy for these failures: "If we confess our sins, he is faithful and just to forgive us our sins and to cleanse us from all unrighteousness" (1 John 1:9). Such failure, however, though possible, is not necessary.

Because of the crucifixion and resurrection of Jesus and the indwelling ministry of the Holy Spirit, we are born again as new people. But we must be diligent to preserve the most important convictions and disciplines in order to see the life of Christ in us flourish. We have a cunning foe, Satan. His desire is to destroy believers in order that God's glory shining through us to others will be diminished. Christ followers cannot be too alert, protective, or disciplined.

Seventh and finally, marriage is meant to be lifelong. Of course, the death of either the man or the woman can cut that short, but the marriage relationship is perhaps one of the few things on this earth that is built to last. Paul addresses this durability of marriage in 1 Corinthians

7:39: "A wife is bound to her husband as long as he lives. But if her husband dies, she is free to be married to whom she wishes, only in the Lord."

Living Out a God-Designed Marriage

God set all the designs and purposes He thought necessary for us to understand in the very beginning of the story—the book of Genesis. These designs not only display His power and glory but His provision as well. In them we find as much comfort, joy, and fulfillment as we can have this side of eternity.

Through a joint commitment to the Scriptures, the husband and wife nurture their relationship with God and remind themselves of His Word's importance. Through it they also protect themselves from the flesh that lingers in their bodies and from Satan, who is "a roaring lion, seeking someone to devour." We must "resist him, firm in [our] faith, knowing that the same kinds of suffering are being experienced by [our] brotherhood throughout the world" (1 Pet. 5:8–9).

In marriage the husband and wife are not two identical people; they are two uniquely different people designed by God and brought together in Him. They will have to navigate many decisions over their lifetime together, so the values they live out, their understanding about who they are in Christ, and why they live must be discussed, understood, and agreed upon. This requires time and dialogue. It also demands a predisposition to want it.

The husband and wife are heirs together, but they are still imperfect. That will be the case until the flesh dies and both man and woman are ushered into an eternity of divine design. But by God's design, even now, they can be heirs together.

chapter 6

THE ETERNAL PROMISE

Because we are created in the image and likeness of God and endowed by Him with the ability to create, will, and manage, we are able to make choices. Adam and Eve chose self over divine design, and that single cataclysmic decision introduced the flesh as the dominating force in all mankind.

At that moment of apparent failure, however, as we have seen, God introduced a saving promise, declaring to the serpent that an offspring of Eve would deliver a fatal blow to his head and that Satan would do nothing more than nip at His heels: "I will put enmity between you and the woman, and between your seed and her Seed; he shall bruise your head, and you shall bruise his heel" (Gen. 3:15, NKJV). This promise of God was released into time and, from the divine-design point of view, has dominated all human history.

This promise has been advanced throughout history by men and women who have cultivated relationship with God and faithfully represented Him in the places where He has led them, and it is still being carried out in our day. This is indeed the call of believers in Jesus Christ—that we partner with God in His mission in the world.

One day the promise will be completely fulfilled, and eternity will restore God's original design for its recipients. But in this era of mercy, the people of God have a part to play in the advancement of God's promise to restore divine design. The promise of God to redeem broken humanity has threaded itself into history, and we are part of that ongoing story.

The Promise Advanced

In the Old Testament Noah, Abraham, David and the prophets were among those who received, believed, and advanced the fulfillment of the promise. Each of them received a unique mission, a small part to play in the fulfillment of the promise that anticipated and advanced the larger promise from God—salvation in Jesus Christ.

To Noah God promised,

Behold, I establish my covenant with you and your offspring after you, and with every living creature that is with you, the birds, the livestock, and every beast of the earth with you, as many as came out of the ark; it is for every beast of the earth. I establish my covenant with you, that never again shall all flesh be cut off by the waters of the flood, and never again shall there be a flood to destroy the earth. (Gen. 9:9–11)

How much Noah understood about the promise of God is unclear to us today, but he understood enough about God and His design to take on God's command for him to build an ark. For many decades he and his family labored at building this floating vessel miles and miles from any body of water that could float it. Noah believed God and obeyed Him in the particular thing He asked him to do.

To Abraham God promised,

Go from your country and your kindred and your father's house to the land that I will show you. And I will make of you a great nation, and I will bless you and make your name great, so that you will be a blessing. I will bless those who bless you, and him who dishonors you I will curse, and in you all the families of the earth shall be blessed. (Gen. 12:1–3)

Abraham had no written Scripture, no body of believers surrounding him to encourage and exhort him, as we in the church do today. All he had were interactions with God and occasional messengers of God who visited him. But Abraham believed God that from his loins and from Sarah's womb, in spite of their advanced ages, a family would be born—and from that family a clan would be born, and from that clan a nation would be born, and from that nation blessing would extend to other nations. Abraham would be the father of many nations.

Paul described just how miraculous this promise was and how faithful Abraham was to it:

In hope he believed against hope, that he should become the father of many nations, as he had been told, "So shall your offspring be." He did not weaken in faith when he considered his own body, which was as good as dead (since he was about a hundred years old), or when he considered the barrenness of Sarah's womb. No unbelief made him waver concerning the promise of God, but he grew strong in his faith as he gave glory to God, fully convinced that God was able to do what he had promised. (Rom. 4:18–21)

To the nation of Israel in the final days of Moses God promised,

Now, O Israel, listen to the statutes and the rules that I am teaching you, and do them, that you may live, and go in and take possession of the land that the Lord, the God of your fathers, is giving you. . . . Keep them and do them, for that will be your wisdom and your understanding in the sight of the peoples, who, when they hear all these statutes, will say, "Surely this great nation is a wise and understanding people." For what great nation is there that has a god so near to it as the Lord our God is to us, whenever we call upon him? (Deut. 4:1–7)

Israel's part in advancing the promise was to obey the law. They were to honor it and live according to it, and their obedient witness and its fruit would draw the nations to the Lord.

To David God promised through the prophet Nathan, "Your house and your kingdom shall be made sure forever before me. Your throne shall be established forever" (2 Sam. 7:16). As in the cases of Noah, Abraham, and many others, David responded in humility and faith: "What more can David say to you? For you know your servant, O Lord God! Because of your promise, and according to your own heart, you have brought about all this greatness, to make your servant know it" (2 Sam. 7:20–21).

To the prophets God made similar promises, in spite of their role in judging and warning the people to turn from faithlessness to faithfulness. He spoke clearly to the prophet Isaiah regarding the nation of Israel,

I will take you by the hand and keep you; I will give you as a covenant for the people, a light for the nations, to open the eyes that are blind, to bring out the prisoners from the dungeon, from the prison those who sit in darkness. (Isa. 42:6–7)

And to Jeremiah,

Behold, the days are coming, declares the Lord, when I will make a new covenant with the house of Israel and the house of Judah. . . . For this is the covenant that I will make with the house of Israel after those days, declares the Lord: I will put my law within them, and I will write it on their hearts. And I will be their God, and they shall be my people. (Jer. 31:31–33)

All these Old Testament people received the greater promise of God as part of a particular promise given to them that required faith on their part. Hebrews is a partial listing of this inspiring "cloud of witnesses" (Heb. 12:1). These men and women received the promise for two reasons. First, they understood that God rewards those who diligently seek Him: "Without faith it is impossible to please him, for whoever would draw near to God must believe that he exists and that he rewards those who seek him" (Heb. 11:6). And second, by their obedience to the partial promise each of them received and their limited understanding of the fuller promise, they demonstrated that they were not really citizens of this earth but were looking for another, more enduring home:

> *These all died in faith, not having received the things promised, but having seen them and greeted them from afar, and having acknowledged that they were strangers and exiles on the earth. For people who speak thus make it clear that they are seeking a homeland. If they had been thinking of that land from which they had gone out, they would have had opportunity to return. But as it is, they desire a better country, that is, a heavenly one. Therefore God is not ashamed to be called their God, for he has prepared for them a city. (Heb. 11:13–16)*

Noah, Abraham, Moses, David, Jeremiah, and many others, named and unnamed, embraced the promise. Some were asked simply to anticipate the promise, like Joseph, who anticipated the restoration of Israel to the Promised Land and demonstrated his faith by requiring that his bones be returned there. Others had to believe that God could raise someone from the dead to ultimately fulfill His promise, as Abraham was when he offered Isaac back to God. Some suffered greatly for their faith in the promise:

> *Others suffered mocking and flogging, and even chains and im-*

prisonment. They were stoned, they were sawn in two, they were killed with the sword. They went about in skins of sheep and goats, destitute, afflicted, mistreated—of whom the world was not worthy—wandering about in deserts and mountains, and in dens and caves of the earth. (Heb. 11:36–38)

But while each of these received and acted upon a different piece of the promise, all of them lived in anticipation of the fulfillment of the original promise of God seen in Genesis 3:15. We are the recipients of God's patience and their witness: "All these, though commended through their faith, did not receive what was promised, since God had provided something better for us, that apart from us they should not be made perfect" (Heb. 11:39–40).

The Promise Fulfilled—and the Believer's Role Given

Only through Jesus did God finally fulfill the promise. Jesus clearly declared this to the disciples at the Last Supper: "He took a cup, and when he had given thanks he gave it to them, saying, 'Drink of it, all of you, for this is my blood of the covenant, which is poured out for many for the forgiveness of sins'" (Matt. 26:27–28). In this same regard Paul wrote to the Galatians, "The Scripture imprisoned everything under sin, so that the promise by faith in Jesus Christ might be given to those who believe" (Gal. 3:22).

Through His death, burial, and resurrection, Jesus gained the authority to restore the original divine design of God in men and women and fulfilled the promise of Genesis 3. With this authority He now sends His re-created people, those who believe in Jesus Christ, into the world to announce this gospel, the good news:

All authority in heaven and on earth has been given to me. Go therefore and make disciples of all nations, baptizing them in the name of the Father and of the Son and of the Holy Spirit, teaching

them to observe all that I have commanded you.
(Matt. 28:18–20)

This is our own small part in the promise! Just as the patriarchs and the prophets of old received a portion of God's promise to redeem lost men and women to Himself, so we too are given a part to play in the great story of history. As believers in Jesus, our call to relationship with God and representation of Him is to live out the gospel message to the people around us in the places where God has called us.

Part 2 of this book will expand on this calling in detail. Through Jesus' words in the Sermon on the Mount, we will see how God is continuing to thread history with His original design and His promise to restore that design—through every follower of Jesus Christ.

Our time is limited, because this era of mercy in which we live will one day come to an end, when Christ will return and judge those who have lived upon the earth. But nothing will be lost to God that He intends to rescue and restore. This motivates us to intentionally grow in our relationship with God and to learn to represent Him in holiness in the days before His return, which is what Paul reminded Titus to do:

The grace of God has appeared, bringing salvation for all people, training us to renounce ungodliness and worldly passions, and to live self-controlled, upright, and godly lives in the present age, waiting for our blessed hope, the appearing of the glory of our great God and Savior Jesus Christ. (Titus 2:11–13)

At the return of Jesus, God will complete the promise! This compels us, the followers of Jesus, to embrace our small part in the promise of redemption—our mission, our calling—and to live in anticipation of the fulfillment of the whole promise.

Since all these things are thus to be dissolved, what sort of people ought you to be in lives of holiness and godliness, waiting for and

> *hastening the coming of the day of God, because of which the heavens will be set on fire and dissolved, and the heavenly bodies will melt as they burn! But according to his promise we are waiting for new heavens and a new earth in which righteousness dwells. (2 Pet. 3:11–13)*

Indeed! What kind of people ought we to be! If we know the end of the story and we are children who belong to the promise, what impact should these things have on our daily lives? According to Peter, we should be people who live holy lives, people who live godly lives, people whose lives anticipate the return of Jesus, and people who build lifestyles that cooperate with Christ's return.

We were re-created for this. But I would be remiss if I simply painted a picture of God's design without also giving the Son of God's description of what it looks like in the believer's daily life. As we go forward, we will examine the revealing picture that Jesus builds of that re-created life in the Sermon on the Mount.

PART TWO

Divine Design in the Follower of Jesus

Blessed are the poor in spirit, for theirs is the kingdom of heaven. Blessed are those who mourn, for they shall be comforted. Blessed are the meek, for they shall inherit the earth. Blessed are those who hunger and thirst for righteousness, for they shall be satisfied. Blessed are the merciful, for they shall receive mercy. Blessed are the pure in heart, for they shall see God. Blessed are the peacemakers, for they shall be called sons of God. Blessed are those who are persecuted for righteousness' sake, for theirs is the kingdom of heaven. Blessed are you when others revile you and persecute you and utter all kinds of evil against you falsely on my account. Rejoice and be glad, for your reward is great in heaven, for so they persecuted the prophets who were before you.

Matthew 5:3–12

chapter 7

GOD'S DESIGN FOR THE BELIEVER IN CHRIST

As I travel the world, I am consistently alarmed at the weak understanding of the gospel I find among Christians. The New Testament is replete with the reality that identification with Jesus also anticipates sanctification. In other words, relationship with God should naturally lead to godly living. Those who submit to the death, burial, and resurrection of Jesus are now capable of living, and are expected to live, as God has re-created us to live: like His Son, Jesus. Instead I find a different reality among believers today.

Organized Christianity today is largely made up of programs—meetings, worship services, small groups, social gatherings. People attend church and get involved in various activities, but in many cases those same people have never truly understood the gospel and been transformed by it. This has led to a great many "faith stillborns," as we noted in chapter 2—people who have verbally received Christ but do not look or act like Him.

In Jesus Christ, believers are new creations. Paul tells us in Ephesians 2:19–22 that we are the temple of the Holy Spirit—each of us part of a new building being built by God as believers, one by one, come to salvation in Him! God is building us, stone by stone, in the various places where He wants us to be. Thus we are sprinkled as rays of gospel light in our neighborhoods and marketplaces throughout the world. It is this sprinkling of people, families, and local churches that the Holy Spirit uses to add to Christ's body each new rock.

One day this ministry of the gospel, lived and spoken by the Spirit through each and every one of Christ's people, will have run its full and complete course (see Matt. 24:14). Until then, it is the maturing distinctiveness of every believer, as members of Christ's larger body, that enables every man, woman, and child their own opportunity to hear and understand God's good news. This is the genetic pattern that God has woven into the very nature of Christ's body—relationship with God leading to representation of God.

The grand yet simple purpose of divine design, however, is too often lost in the overly structured institution that so many today call the church. But God has only had one purpose from the very beginning, and it has been working itself through history ever since Adam and Eve sinned—the restoration of men and women to divine design as first promised in Genesis 3:15. And He has one instrument for accomplishing this restoration—His people. None can be left out of the living and telling of the Gospel story. No one is insignificant in this task. No one is dispensable!

I myself didn't always understand this design of God's for His people. By the time I was in my thirties, Patti and I had spent more than ten years in ministry, first in a local American church and later as missionaries in Latin America. Following that I served as an associate pastor in a growing church in Southern California. I was living out my dream, preaching the Word, and seeing hundreds of people added to the body.

But God invaded my success and forced me to ask where are all these people were coming from—and the findings made me uncomfortable. Much of our growth was due to people transferring from other churches, and often people who did respond to an invitation for salvation were gone from the church within six months. We as God's people were not truly making an impact on the area in which we lived. I was forced to dig into the Word, and when I did, I found divine design looking me squarely in the face. It wasn't my work as a leader or our church's programs that were going to make a difference in our city—it was the people of God living transformed, sanctified lives in the various places where God had called each one of them.

As important as preaching, worship, small groups, and even evangelism are, they are not the primary calling of God's people. The body of Christ does need structure, but when structure leads to institution, and when institutional significance trumps the empowering of Christ's people to live out God's divine design in their marketplaces, then we have succumbed to sin. Worse, we have cut off the single-most important instrument besides the Holy Spirit that God has to engage the world with His grace message: people!

Whatever God is going to do in the neighborhoods, cities, states, and even nations of the world, He is going to do through each and every one of Christ's people. This calls local churches to be directly involved in going, sending, participating, cooperating, and being held accountable for the extension of the gospel.

Understanding this is important, because the Western idea of church has been exported, for hundreds of years, all over the globe. The seed we possess is the only one we can reproduce. If we as believers in Christ are going to effectively take the gospel to the world, the seed we possess must be biblical and lead to reproduction, not addition and maintenance.

The Sanctified Believer

In the introduction to the Revelation, the apostle John says, "To Him who loves us and released us from our sins by His blood . . . He has made us to be a kingdom, priests to His God and Father" (Rev. 1:5–6, NASB). What exactly do these two key phrases describing believers mean? This is important, because these two truths contain the foundation of the gospel—God's story that has been unfolding since the creation.

First, we have been "released from our sins" and reconciled to God through our acceptance of Jesus' death and resurrection. When we receive the gospel, or believe in Jesus, as the Lord stated in John 3:16, God restores us to a right relationship with Himself. As the writer of Hebrews says so clearly in chapters 9–10, we are given a clean conscience, and because of that we can come boldly into the presence of God (see Heb. 4:14–16)!

This new relationship with God ushers us into a new representation of God: we are made a kingdom of priests. Priests stand between people and God. The Old Testament priest regularly represented Israel before God, chiefly through the administration of the sacrifices of the people, but in the New Testament, the new temple is found within followers of Jesus as they are indwelt by God the Holy Spirit. As priests before God, He puts us into new relationship with people who are out of relationship with Him, and we become His representation to the world.

Believers in Christ are not the only representation of God to the world—God has revealed Himself in nature, in the Mosaic law, in Christ, and He daily reaches out to the world through the Holy Spirit, who is convincing the world of "sin and righteousness and judgment" (John 16:8). But the God who is on mission to redeem men and women to Himself and who is using all human history to complete that mission reclaims His Jesus children as instruments in this task.

Our salvation in Jesus and the resident Holy Spirit working in and through the whole of our lives create the primary conduits for our representation of God in the world. As Paul says in Ephesians 1:23, we as believers are the fullness of Him who fills everything in every way. Justification (salvation) anticipates sanctification (increasing holiness), and both will eventually lead to ultimate glorification (see Rom. 8:29–30). This is the New Testament gospel. Any message that does not clearly declare this and any believer who does not anticipate it is walking a dangerous path.

Missio Dei—on Mission with God

Many believers today have wandered from what holy men and women throughout history have understood from Scripture about the purpose and life of the Jesus community. Many Christians have ignored, forgotten, or even demeaned the calling and convictions of multitudes across two thousand years who have given themselves to God's mission—completing the last sending command of their Lord and Savior Jesus Christ: "In your going make disciples of all the peoples of the world" (Matt. 28:19, translation mine).

My life as a young man was formed by Scripture and by the Holy Spirit through godly parents, Christian community, ministry experience, and a few very important evangelization-committed mentors who spent their lives thinking on and seeking to obey this last command of Jesus. These people consistently pointed me to Scripture as my foundation and motivation. My mentors were leaders who understood that evangelism today must be rooted in the beginning of the biblical story.

The storyline of the Bible, as we have seen, is quite simple. God created men and women in His own image, designing us to relate to Him and represent Him by active stewardship of the world He had created and in which He placed us. From Adam and Eve's failure onward, God took man's restoration into His own hands, and the storyline of redemption unfolds across the pages of Scripture. In simple terms, mercy is the centrality of that unfolding. Because of God's mercy and unilateral action in Jesus through the Spirit, grace is extended to sinful man. Now, through the death, burial, and resurrection of God's Son, Jesus, men and women can be restored to the image of God as He originally intended. Still, we still struggle with our sin nature in this fallen world. At the end of this world, however, righteousness will be fully restored in those who believe in Christ as well as in the whole of the new world. In that day righteousness will reign, and men will grow and mature in God's design for them—relationship with Him and representation of Him.

As many previous generations of God's people have understood, God is on a mission—*missio Dei*—and we, the already redeemed ones, are servants in this mission. When we are related to God on a daily basis through His Word and as a result represent Him in our particular and unique stewardship here on Earth, we glorify Him.

Paul declares this in Ephesians 3:10–11: "Through the church the manifold wisdom of God [is now] made known to the rulers and authorities in the heavenly places. This was according to the eternal purpose that he has realized in Christ Jesus our Lord." Eternity is an audience of the miraculous actions of God in Jesus, and the church is God's present instrument for displaying this reality to spiritual rulers and authorities. Our mission as believers has its focus not on time but on eternity. It is rooted in God's eternal purpose.

Believers today do not need to be kept busy with church programs; rather, we need to remember that the church is not the story but that God in His redemptive action is the story, and the church is God's instrument for transmitting His redemptive action to the rest of His creation. A wandering generation needs to be reminded that church leadership exists to move us as believers fully and faithfully in this God design—the body as a whole and each believer as a member in it.

If we as believers in Christ are going to strategically apply the gospel in each and every context of our world, we need to recall the example and teaching of generations of faithful followers who sought to represent God with their part in God's promise of restoration. This teaching is not new. In my nearly fifty years of participating in this stewardship, I can trace at least three generations who went before my colleagues and me and from whom we have learned.

More than fifty years ago men like Kenneth Strachan, evangelist and general director of the Latin America Mission, were talking about saturation evangelism—God's people living incarnational lives among the people and in the places where He calls them. If we concentrated our efforts together for a specific time in a specific place, he asked, could we see the task of taking the gospel to all the earth completed?

Many believers learned and accomplished much through his innovations, but much was still missing.

The next generation, however, extended his teaching. I was stimulated to think and learn from men like Donald McGavran, founder of the Fuller School of World Mission, who called his students to think about people movements; Ralph Winter, missiologist and founder of U.S. Center for World Mission and other missions institutions, who called his students to think about how many peoples exist in the world and how far they are from being reached; and Jim Montgomery, founder of Dawn Ministries, who desired to saturate people and places with the knowledge of God and asked if this could be more effectively accomplished by having a church planted in every small place.

Many more brought their own nuances and additions to these ideas, and my generation learned. Indeed, in recent decades the growth of the church of Jesus Christ all over the world has been unprecedented. When I began my own journey in this stewardship in the late 1960s, many Christians felt as if the glass of evangelization was half empty. Today I rejoice to be part of a generation that is seeing fulfilled what so many others dreamed of and sacrificed to see come about!

Across my lifetime large gatherings and their resulting movements have been used by God to contribute to the blessing we see unfolding today. In some ways the World Congress on Evangelism in Berlin in 1966 kicked off a series of movements; Jim Montgomery cited this conference as the beginning of his search for a whole-nation church-planting strategy. The Lausanne Movement and its gatherings of the 1970s and '80s called men and women from all over the world to live out the gospel in their unique marketplaces and created a new consciousness about the world and what it would take to reach that world. By the year 2000 the Alliance for Saturation Church Planting, the unreached-peoples movement, and many more associations came into being to extend the missio Dei design of God to the ends of the earth.

This short fifty-year review is only a small part of similar movements that have marched across the two-thousand-year life of the church on Earth. In every generation certain men and women have understood the purpose of the church and have taken the gospel to their own places and to the world far from them. Believers today do not stand alone—we are a succeeding generation that God is using to continue to fulfill His mission. We stand upon the shoulders of many others, learning from them and extending what we learn in order to see God's mission of redemption in this world completed and the world of righteousness come!

The apostles began the task, with Thomas reaching as far as India and Paul evangelizing the whole of the Roman Empire. The work was continued across the first several hundred years through people like Polycarp, Ulfilas, Patrick, and Columba. The Roman Catholic Church was not without people who understood the apostolic sending nature of the church—Boniface, Raymond Lull, Matthew Ricci, and many others gave their lives to carrying the gospel to the world. The Moravians led the way in the early days after the Protestant Reformation, and they established the modern missionary movement. And in the years following the Reformation, the church and the missio Dei designs of God were more closely intertwined than they had been in the past.

As we have emphasized, whatever God is going to do in the world, He is going to do through all Christ's people. Individual believers working in unity in the body are God's genius design for declaring to the world and to principalities and rulers in heavenly places that men and women are created for Him. God will not be thwarted. His original designs will be accomplished in the people He restores to Himself through the death, burial, and resurrection of His Son, Jesus Christ.

Investing Our Lives in the Kingdom of God

The central message of the gospel, as we have noted repeatedly, is that men, women, and children can be restored to the original designs of God in Adam and Eve. Believers in Christ Jesus are restored to relationship with God through the death, burial, and resurrection of His

Son, the last Adam, as we receive God's forgiveness, restoration, and an eternal inheritance. We are also restored to representation of God as we take on His design. We become the incarnation of the mercy message that God has completed in Jesus in every place where the Holy Spirit daily leads us, and our lives become one of the most evident proofs that the gospel has power to heal the sin condition of man.

The Christian life is meant to be invested in the kingdom of God as an act of worship, but in order to effectively invest it, it must be worth investing. In other words, as believers in restored relationship with God, we must be growing in sanctification and on fruitful mission with Him.

This transformation of our lives and the resulting investment in God's kingdom comes when the indwelling Holy Spirit uses our regular, submissive interaction with God in His Word. And, because God created us to be part of the body of Christ, it comes in miraculous association with others like us whom God has made His own: the church.

God has designed His people to look like Him! This is the central message of the chapters that follow as we look at the Sermon on the Mount and the dramatic words of Jesus to His followers. They are dramatic to the world, but they should be comfortable to Christ's followers—especially when we realize that they reveal the designs God has planned from before the beginning.

chapter 8

RELATIONSHIP LEADS TO REPRESENTATION

According to the apostle Paul in his letter to Titus, "the grace of God has appeared" (Titus 2:11). Yet imagine the frustration of generations of obedient Christians to the apparent definitiveness of this statement against the reality that so many people in the world do not know Christ! In 1901 Andrew Murray reflected on this dichotomy, "Of all the mysteries that surround us in the world, is not one of the strangest and most incomprehensible this—that after 1800 years the very name of the Son of God should be unknown to the larger half of the human race."[1]

But 2016 is radically different from 1901. The prayers of generations of faithful Christians devoted to the spread of the gospel, though not completely answered, have been and are being answered in miraculous ways.

Nothing is more significant and important to the spread of the gospel than that for the first time in two thousand years, the church of Jesus Christ today is both global and international. All the rules of engagement about world evangelization—where it is done and who does it—are irrevocably changing. Nearly forty years ago church historian Kenneth Latourette pointed out,

Since it had its birth, its first triumphs, and its initial chief stronghold in the Graeco-Roman world, Christianity was profoundly molded by it. In organization and in thought it conformed in part to it. It came to be largely identified with what is called the Occident, that portion of mankind which is the heir of Greece, Rome, and itself. Only occasionally did it spread extensively among non-Occidental peoples. Not until recently has it gained substantial footing in all the other great cultural units and among the majority of the primitive groups of mankind. Only within the past few decades has it become actually world-wide.[2]

Not only is the church of Jesus truly global for the first time in its two-thousand-year odyssey, but it is truly international. The expansion of the church to so many people all over the world has truly been extraordinary. In Latin America, for example, the church today exceeds one hundred million followers of Jesus. The continent of South America alone is an incarnated witness of the power of the gospel and the extraordinary expansion orchestrated by the Holy Spirit even in my short lifetime.

When my wife, Patti, and I first went to Latin America in the early 1970s, few expected to see the expansion of the church that we have seen over the years. In fact, one veteran missionary told me just before we left Latin America in the late '70s, as he was retiring from the field, that he felt like Moses, having wasted forty years of his life in the wilderness. But today in the very country where both of us labored during a good part of the twentieth century, local churches of tens of thousands of cell groups and hundreds of thousands of followers of Jesus have become a reality.

When the doors to China first slammed shut to the normal missionary ministry of the gospel in the early 1950s, we counted no more than one million followers of Jesus there—and that growth had taken thousands of missionaries and at least 150 years! When the political tundra of relationship between China and the West first began to thaw in the early 1970s, some reported as many as fifty million followers of Jesus in China, and many today say that there are approaching a hundred million followers of Jesus there. What little we can see through the veil of Communist government tells us that we are witnessing from afar the fullness of the story of Acts in that land.

This story can be repeated on every continent of the world. The gospel of Jesus has gone out with power over the last two hundred years of the modern missionary movement from the West to the rest. The number of believers in America pales in comparison to the aggregate followers of Jesus around the world and even in comparison to some national churches in the world. What we have prayed for has come to pass! Grace has indeed appeared to us!

Understanding True Salvation

But what do this powerful witness of the grace of God and these words of Paul to Titus say to us today? Paul gives us the answer: "The grace of God has appeared, bringing salvation" (Titus 2:11)! We who are believers in Jesus have indeed received salvation, and as men and women re-created in the image of God, we are to take this salvation to the world.

The salvation to which Paul refers, however, is important for us to understand as believers on mission with God, lest we lead people and ourselves to misunderstand salvation from God's declared Word. Dallas Willard touches on this danger that has affected much of the church in the twentieth and twenty-first centuries:

> Much of evangelism today is rooted in a misunderstanding of salvation. People have been told they are Christians because they have confessed they believe that Jesus died for their sins, but the total package is presented in such a way that it leaves the general life untouched.

Biblically, salvation means deliverance—the question is, "Deliverance from what?" The common message is "deliverance from guilt." But the full concept of salvation in the New Testament is deliverance from our present sins. Deliverance from sins comes from the new life of God's kingdom when we place our confidence in Jesus the person. The problem is that we have been obsessed with this idea that the real issue is "making the cut" to get to heaven. We have taken the discipleship out of conversion.[3]

God's salvation is not an escape from hell or a delivery to heaven; it is a restoration of people to Himself and to His divine design for them. As a result, salvation is a delivering from sin to righteousness, from alienation from God to friendship with God, from the kingdom of darkness to the kingdom of light. Because it is a restoration of relationship to God, it touches the totality of who we are as human beings and is the starting point of our transformation into the image of God's Son, Jesus Christ, the perfect example of human life as God originally designed it.

Paul explains that this salvation is for "all people" (Titus 2:11). The apostle Peter adds, "The Lord is not slow in keeping his promise, as some understand slowness. Instead he is patient with you, not wanting anyone to perish, but everyone to come to repentance" (2 Pet. 3:8–9, NIV). In Peter's words we see the design of God developing throughout history and how He is orchestrating it for His purposes and His glory.

Those who receive this salvation are then to "say 'No' to ungodliness and worldly passions, and to live self-controlled, upright and godly lives in this present age" (Titus 2:12, NIV). The life of a genuine believer will evidence holiness.

Finally, this salvation leads us to wait "for our blessed hope, the appearing of the glory of our great God and Savior Jesus Christ" (Titus 2:13). Philip Towner, of the American Bible Society, says of the present gospel and the future it anticipates, "The present age, and life in it, thus takes its meaning from these two reference points. The past reference point is certain, historical; it is the substance of the gospel message. The future reference point is based on the past event, but its time is uncertain, requiring hope and the expectant forward look."[4]

Paul has explained what this salvation is, but now he goes on to give us several reasons why God has saved us. He has saved us, first of all, "to redeem us from all lawlessness" (Titus 2:14)! Paul expands on this thought in Ephesians 4:17–24:

> *I tell you this, and insist on it in the Lord, that you must no longer live as the Gentiles do, in the futility of their thinking. They are darkened in their understanding and separated from the life of God because of the ignorance that is in them due to the hardening of their hearts. Having lost all sensitivity, they have given themselves over to sensuality so as to indulge in every kind of impurity, and they are full of greed.*

> *That, however, is not the way of life you learned when you heard about Christ and were taught in him in accordance with the truth that is in Jesus. You were taught, with regard to your former way of life, to put off your old self, which is being corrupted by its deceitful desires; to be made new in the attitude of your minds; and to put on the new self, created to be like God in true righteousness and holiness. (NIV)*

Further, we are saved because God wanted "to purify for himself a people for his own possession" (Titus 2:14). This truth, so clear in the Bible, is in antagonism to the culture we live in and to all human history and experience. People want to belong to themselves, not to another, and surely not to God. But God's desire to purify a people for His own possession is the story of creation; it was the story of the Old Testament; it's the story of the gospel. Of this purification inherent in divine design, Towner comments that through this washing in Jesus,

God is purifying a people for Himself, claiming them out of their sin and former rebellion.

Finally, Paul writes to Titus, we are saved to be "zealous for good works" (Titus 2:14). We are to be always on the lookout for what we have been created to do! "We are his workmanship, created in Christ Jesus for good works, which God prepared beforehand, that we should walk in them" (Eph. 2:10).

Growing Progressively in Our Salvation

This salvation that has appeared to us in Jesus Christ can be seen as a journey. As messengers of this gospel message to the world, we must realize that we are to progressively live out our salvation as we continue in relationship to Him and represent Him in the world He has made for us to steward. As we grow in our salvation, our witness of Christ will grow as well.

The Sermon on the Mount is an outline of our salvation in Christ—of divine design in the believer—and it reveals not so much how our lives are to be lived but how they are to be expressed to the world around us! The broad outline in the Sermon on the Mount shows us the journey of progressive relationship and growing representation that God designed for us and then re-created in those of us who are in Jesus Christ. It reveals how we can increasingly demonstrate God's righteousness in all the places toward all the people and in all the vocations where God leads us.

The Sermon on the Mount begins with a description of God's re-created people in the Beatitudes and shows how distinctive we are from the rest of the world (see Matt. 5:1–12). As men and women saved by God, we live in ways that surprise and contradict the patterns of those held in bondage to sin and Satan. We are blessed when we are poor in spirit, and we rejoice when we are persecuted. God's people are designed to be dramatically different from those around us—those who are dominated by the sin they inherited from their fathers and mothers, by the world that works to entice their sin nature into rebellion against God at every turn, and by Satan, who loves to see human beings in disobedience to God and His designs. All true children of God look like their Father in heaven. He is a Father of righteousness!

The Sermon on the Mount goes on to show how important God's people are to His plan for human history (see Matt. 5:13–20). As "the salt of the earth" (Matt. 5:13), we preserve the image of God in a fallen world. We retain the dignity of what it means to be human in a world in which so many treat others as sub-human, and thus we remind the world that the Creator God did not create man to demean others. We are "the light of the world" (Matt. 5:14), showing the way to godliness for those who want to see. High on a hill, we direct the way to the living God, calling all to see His glory and shedding light on the world's corruption, self-centeredness, arrogance, greed, and perversion. God's children also convey truth, for we obey and teach the commandments of God, having founded our lives on the only unfailing truth in the world, the Word of God. Our righteousness is not built on the external actions of religious obligation but upon the transformed nature that we have received from our Father in heaven. As a result, our "righteousness exceeds that of the scribes and Pharisees" (Matt. 5:20).

Jesus goes on to teach that the life of a person who has been truly saved stands in stark contrast to those who live by the world's standards (see Matt. 5:21–48). God's righteousness comes not from external conformity but from the new birth in Jesus Christ, the transforming power of the Word of God, and the empowering presence of the Holy Spirit within us. Therefore, murder, adultery, divorce, oaths, revenge, and retaliation are foreign to the lifestyles of God's children. Understanding the image of God within every man, we learn from the Word and the Spirit how to treat people differently, whether that be our brother, our spouse, someone of the opposite gender, a stranger, or even our enemy. We understand God's control over our lives and human history and depend upon that rather than the useless bluster that comes with human oaths.

The sermon next speaks of proactive goodness—positive actions that are the result of God's salvation working in us (see Matt. 6:1–7:6). For example, when we give, we do so as if our right hand did not know what our left was doing. When we pray, we understand that God is listening, and we are fully focused upon Him alone. When we fast, the people around us have a hard time realizing it. We invest in the kingdom of God, trusting God to provide for our needs even before we ask Him to! We realize that God is the only true and just judge, so as peacemakers, we let Him do the judging.

Finally, since we have been made new, we discover new spiritual disciplines to live by (see Matt. 7:7–27), developing discernment as we grow in prayer and in the Word of God. This progressive growth in the life of someone who has received Christ's salvation reflects the promise of another world in eternity in which God will completely restore all that He created in the beginning.

Living Out Our Salvation

In the Sermon on the Mount, God's expectations for His children saved by grace are summed up in a simple phrase: "You therefore must be perfect, as your heavenly Father is perfect" (Matt. 5:48). In other words, as we have noted before, "Be like your Father, because you now have His seed and His Spirit living in you."

In the Sermon on the Mount, Jesus gives us a description of life as God first created it to be, in His image and likeness, and also as He intends it to be in the new world of righteousness to come. His words are not idle words. They are our life. As such, we must know and embrace them. We must carry them with us as Israel did with their phylacteries on their foreheads and arms. We must contemplate them. Ultimately, we must obey them, for they are our life.

This grace that has appeared in the Son of God, Jesus Christ, and that we are to progressively grow in, is for the world we live in today— and you and I are the primary instruments God will use to let people see and hear about it. As God inhabits His people through His Holy Spirit, the Holy Spirit will transform us into the image of our Savior, Jesus Christ, and our lives will tell the story of the gospel.

chapter 9

GOD'S PEOPLE AND THEIR IMPORTANCE TO HIS MISSION

All too often we fail to realize just how important God's children are to His kingdom. As the obedient ones who have been transformed by the death, burial, and resurrection of God's Son, Jesus Christ, we are a living demonstration of life as God designed it. Jesus begins His Sermon on the Mount by describing this life in God's people, showing just how different divine design in the believer is from the world's thinking and patterns (see Matt. 5:1–12). He goes on to describe the potential impact on the world of those who live this life (see Matt. 5:13–20)—those of us who are being transformed by the Holy Spirit.

The People of God

Who are the people of God? What do they look like? The opening verses of the Sermon on the Mount, what many call the Beatitudes, give us a concise picture.

The people of God turn the world's way of thinking upside down. The world's distorted idea of appropriate human behavior is in complete contradiction to God's original divine design for His children and His re-creation of us in Jesus by the Holy Spirit:

Blessed are the poor in spirit, for theirs is the kingdom of heaven. Blessed are those who mourn, for they shall be comforted. Blessed are the meek, for they shall inherit the earth. Blessed are those who hunger and thirst for righteousness, for they shall be satisfied. Blessed are the merciful, for they shall receive mercy. Blessed are the pure in heart, for they shall see God. Blessed are the peacemakers, for they shall be called sons of God. Blessed are those who are persecuted for righteousness' sake, for theirs is the kingdom of heaven. Blessed are you when others revile you and persecute you and utter all kinds of evil against you falsely on my account. Rejoice and be glad, for your reward is great in heaven, for so they persecuted the prophets who were before you. (Matt. 5:1–12)

In the world's opinion, conversely, blessed are the wealthy, for they possess the earth. Blessed are the happy, for they enjoy life. Blessed are the aggressive, for they inherit the fullness of the earth. Blessed are those who hunger to possess, for they are never full and therefore deserve all they can get. Blessed are the self-righteous, for they show no mercy and thereby make sure all their rights are protected. And in a total distortion, blessed are the corrupt, for they don't want to see God. Why would they? They already have all they think they want in personal freedom. Blessed are those who sow division, for they are the sons of man and of the devil. When one can divide, one can conquer, or so the proverb goes. Blessed are the self-protected, for theirs is the kingdom. Blessed are you if you are always liked, for is not that what life is all about?

But God created the earth, and indeed us, to be different from the tainted world system we live in. The qualities He gives us stem from our new birth in Jesus, from the healing found in the Word, and from the empowering of the Holy Spirit who dwells in us, and these cause us to think differently than the world does.

The people of God are "poor in spirit" (Matt. 5:3). This begins when we recognize our need for someone outside ourselves to overcome our inherent failure to be and act as God wants His children to be and act. This realization of incompleteness causes us to "mourn" (Matt. 5:4) over our lost state and become "meek" (Matt. 5:5) and quiet before God, to whom we look for healing.

Because God has called us to Himself, we "hunger and thirst for righteousness" (Matt. 5:6), or wholeness, so that we will not be left "exposed" before God "to whom we must give account" (Heb. 4:13). Having received mercy, we are "merciful" (Matt. 5:7) to others, realizing that but for God's grace we too would be lost.

Having been purified by the blood of Jesus Christ, we become "pure in heart" (Matt. 5:8), with clean motives:

> *If the blood of goats and bulls, and the sprinkling of defiled persons with the ashes of a heifer, sanctify for the purification of the flesh, how much more will the blood of Christ, who through the eternal Spirit offered himself without blemish to God, purify our conscience from dead works to serve the living God.*
> *(Heb. 9:13–14)*

Having received peace with God, we become "peacemakers" (Matt. 5:9). God our Father makes no mistake with our lives, so we can freely give ourselves to others, unconcerned by any potential usurping of our lives by unscrupulous people.

Because we live in a world that is hostile to God, His designs, and His desires, just as Jesus did, we are harassed for being whole, or "persecuted for righteousness' sake" (Matt. 5:10). The world would be more comfortable with us if we were as filthy, destitute, and rebellious as it is, but because we are not, we suffer the persecutions of a world in opposition to God. Because of our allegiance to God and His Son, Jesus Christ, people reject us and "persecute" us and "utter all kinds of evil" (Matt. 5:11) about us.

The Blessings of the People of God

But life for the believer is not all difficult. As the people of God, our Father has prepared for us reward. Those who seek to fulfill their own desires receive in this world the fruits of their decisions—and at the end of this life, they will receive separation from God in the place of the rebellious (see Matt. 25:41). Conversely, while we may be poor in this world, we receive "the kingdom of heaven" (Matt. 5:3) now and will receive it more fully when Jesus returns: "In my Father's house are many rooms. If it were not so, would I have told you that I go to prepare a place for you? And if I go and prepare a place for you, I will come again and will take you to myself, that where I am you may be also" (John 14:2–4).

We are "comforted" (Matt. 5:4) in our lost state, because we now receive the acceptance and affirmation of our heavenly Father: "By a single offering [Christ] has perfected for all time those who are being sanctified" (Heb. 10:14). Those who come to the Father through Christ are made fully accepted by His blood and begin to be made like Him by the Holy Spirit.

We are given the earth to enjoy (see Matt. 5:5) and, more importantly, to steward as God's representatives: "They are to do good, to be rich in good works, to be generous and ready to share, thus storing up treasure for themselves as a good foundation for the future, so that they may take hold of that which is truly life" (1 Tim. 6:18–19).

We are whole and thus "satisfied" (Matt. 5:6). People in the world around us are full of hurt and pain, marred and unhealed by the sin they inherited from their fathers, and they obey the sin nature that is within them. But the people of the kingdom, after the image of our Savior, are being transformed into God's righteous image: "We all, with unveiled face, beholding the glory of the Lord, are being transformed into the same image from one degree of glory to another. For this comes from the Lord who is the Spirit" (2 Cor. 3:18).

Because we have been crucified, buried, and resurrected with Jesus, we "receive mercy" (Matt. 5:7). Romans 11:30–32 expands this thought:

> *Just as you were at one time disobedient to God but now have received mercy because of their disobedience, so they too have now been disobedient in order that by the mercy shown to you they also may now receive mercy. For God has consigned all to disobedience, that he may have mercy on all.*

Through all this we "see God" (Matt. 5:8) and understand His giving nature! "Oh, the depth of the riches and wisdom and knowledge of God! How unsearchable are his judgments and how inscrutable his ways" (Rom. 11:33).

The people of the kingdom are called "sons of God" (Matt. 5:9), even though we do not yet know the full extent of all that we will receive: "We are God's children now, and what we will be has not yet appeared; but we know that when he appears we shall be like him, because we shall see him as he is" (1 John 3:2).

While doubt plagues us in the face of persecution, we receive validation of our faith as we look at the prophets of old, "for so they persecuted the prophets who were before" us (Matt. 5:12):

> *Time would fail me to tell of Gideon, Barak, Samson, Jephthah, of David and Samuel and the prophets—who through faith conquered kingdoms, enforced justice, obtained promises, stopped the mouths of lions, quenched the power of fire, escaped the edge of the sword, were made strong out of weakness, became mighty in war, put foreign armies to flight. Women received back their dead by resurrection. Some were tortured, refusing to accept release, so that they might rise again to a better life. Others suffered mocking and flogging, and even chains and imprisonment. They were stoned, they were sawn in two, they were killed with the sword. They went about in skins of sheep and goats, destitute, af-*

flicted, mistreated—of whom the world was not worthy—wandering about in deserts and mountains, and in dens and caves of the earth. (Heb. 11:32–38)

The lives of the people of the kingdom demonstrate the divine design: we are newly born of a new seed and belong to a new Father—our heavenly Father. We are living witnesses of the truth that life as God designed it is different from what the world understands and knows. We live by the new birth that comes through the death, burial, and resurrection of Jesus Christ by the indwelling ministry of God's Spirit who lives in His children.

The Importance of God's People to His Mission

Having defined the people of God as utterly different from the people of the world, Jesus now makes clear how important this unique life we live is to His mission of restoration.

God's people are "the salt of the earth" (Matt. 5:13). What is it about salt that makes it comparable to the potential impact of God's people upon the world around them? First, salt preserves. People who are the salt of the earth penetrate the earth and preserve whatever degree of God's likeness remains in people.

The impact of sin upon the human experience has marred its beauty, and if left totally unchecked, sin can so corrupt the human experience that the image of God the Creator is all but lost to the human eye, so much so that Paul wrote, "None is righteous, no, not one; no one understands" (Rom. 3:10–11).

Still, the beauty and genius of God is seen in many people. Man is capable of great creative genius, concern for others, and, at times, even sacrifice. In cultures in which there has been an influence of the biblical message, one can note attitudes and actions in people that reflect the genius of God in His human creation, even in those who do not know Him.

But when men, women, and children are born again by the death and resurrection of the Son, they begin a lifetime of restoring and releasing in this world characteristics of God's original design, especially as seen in the life of Jesus. As they spend time in God's Word and submit to the transformation and direction of the Holy Spirit now resident in them, they progressively take on a renewed image and likeness of their Creator and re-Creator, which will one day be fully restored in the new heaven and the new earth. As a result, they are a living witness of how God created the world to be and how it will be again someday. Non-believers should see in us the redeemed and being-made-new life of our Creator. The witness can inspire or convict them, but it should be evident.

Second, salt has the potential to heal. My grandmother taught me this when I was young. Having cut my leg on barbed wire, she sprinkled salt into my wound. It was painful, but it brought healing. The children of God are a healing force within this world of pain, oppression, anger, and brokenness.

All around us the effects of the flesh, the world, and the devil wreak havoc on the human experience—at times so much so that one is left to wonder whether some men are more beasts than human. All over the world, women and children most suffer this havoc. They are oppressed, enslaved, raped, beaten, and starved, often with government and religious leaders looking the other way or even benefiting from their treatment. Take away the "God created us" message, and just about any treatment of others by those more powerful is tolerated.

As the people of the kingdom remind the world of the original intentions of God and through their lives declare that plan, they bring healing to those wracked by the havoc of a world rebellious to God's design. That is the clear message of Jesus: "Truly, I say to you, as you did it to one of the least of these my brothers, you did it to me. . . . As you did not do it to one of the least of these, you did not do it to me" (Matt. 25:40–45). James too reminds us that God calls His children to act on behalf of the unprotected: "Religion that is pure and undefiled before

God, the Father, is this: to visit orphans and widows in their affliction, and to keep oneself unstained from the world" (Jas 1:27).

The children of God, realizing how important their saltiness is to the plan of God, must do all they can to preserve it by spending time listening to God in His Word and then responding in submission to the direction of the Holy Spirit. We must actively fill our minds with the words of God so that our hearts are tender toward God and our wills prepared to act in obedience and submission to Him. If the children of God lose this flavor, they are no longer fit for the purposes for which God designed their presence in His world and are thrown out and trampled by men. We might say that they are made irrelevant to the world in which they live. The gospel is marginalized and the church rejected.

God's people are also "the light of the world" (Matt. 5:14). God's people shine revelation, conviction, and hope into the world. As we live the truths of the kingdom of God through the life-giving power of salvation in Jesus and the empowering of the Holy Spirit, the message of mercy in the gospel is seen by the world.

That lived-out message, accompanied with declaration and explanation, brings revelation about God to the people living around us. God's mercy message, begun before time even existed, still demands response in the world today: "He chose us in [Christ] before the foundation of the world, that we should be holy and blameless before him" (Eph. 1:4). When the knowledge of this message is interpreted by the Spirit in the lives of observers and hearers, conviction and new life can result from the sovereign act of God. For those who repent and embrace the new birth available in the life, death, and resurrection of Jesus Christ, hope is the result.

Again, as we realize the importance of God's light in us to His purposes, as children of God, we must be vigilant to preserve our light and make it easily observable. The light, like the salt, is maintained by the Spirit of God, but we must cooperate with Him by living daily in the Word of God and obeying what the Spirit says to us through it.

Finally, God's people are the incarnation of truth in the world. Our Master came to fulfill the whole revelation of God laid out for us in the Old Testament, and this revelation is so important to God that those who set aside the truth are "least in the kingdom of heaven" (Matt. 5:19). Those who practice and teach it, however, are great.

The Pharisees and other religious leaders put enormous emphasis upon following the Mosaic law as well as other laws invented by men. But the righteousness of the children of God must exceed the outwardly religious (see Matt. 5:20). Our righteousness exceeds the righteousness of the Pharisees not because we are more active in maintaining religion but because ours is a different kind of righteousness. The righteousness of the Pharisees comes from man; the righteousness of the children of God comes from the new seed that the Father has put in us: "You therefore must be perfect, as your heavenly Father is perfect" (Matt. 5:48). That new seed of life within us looks like our Father.

True righteousness is not mere outward conformity but comes from a new inner reality—being born again!

The Life of the Father in Us

Who we are and how we live is extremely important to the revelation of God's glory in this world, because through our lives we show God's very nature. We are decidedly and uniquely different from the world; we are salt, we are light, we are God's truth. But we must cooperate with this new life: we must preserve our saltiness by regular time in God's Word and submission to the active direction of God's Spirit, and we must not hide our light but allow it to shine every place we go.

chapter 10

RIGHTEOUSNESS VS. ANGER

Having laid the groundwork for how we as God's people are to live in this world as we represent Him, Jesus begins to make some contrasts between the people of God and those who seek to live by this world's system, or, more explicitly, by a strict religious system. The expectations of Jesus for those of us who are related to Him and called to represent Him are not connected to religiosity and its comfort with humanly created rules and obligations, as we see clearly expressed in Jesus' continuing Sermon on the Mount in Matthew 5:21–26.

The Pharisees were well versed in this kind of "human righteousness," but they should have known better, for God had been clear in His Word that He was more concerned with their hearts than their formal outward forms of obedience. Of this truth in the Old Testament Scriptures, nineteenth-century preacher Charles Mackintosh wrote,

> There is immense power in Samuel's brief but pointed reply to Saul, "Hath the Lord as great delight in burnt offerings and sacrifices, as in obeying the voice of the Lord! Behold, to obey is better than sacrifice, and to hearken than the fat of rams" (1 Sam. 15:22). Saul's word was, "Sacrifice." Samuel's word was, "Obedience." No doubt, the bleating of sheep and the lowing

of the oxen were most exciting. They would be looked upon as substantial proofs that something was being done; while on the other hand, the path of obedience seemed narrow, silent, lonely, and fruitless.[1]

Despite God's instruction, we sons and daughters of Adam are always more comfortable with a religion that is controllable by human effort. This allows us to give as much as we think fit and still believe that we are good people and will surely be accepted by God. But the Bible is not a story about religion. It is a story that consumes the whole of human origin, definition, and history.

The Bible is clear: the story of human history is God extending mercy to the rebellious children of Adam and Eve in order to restore some of them to His original design. What the first Adam was unable to accomplish, the last Adam, Jesus Christ, the Son of God, accomplished, and those who are found in Him are restored to God's divine design—relationship with God their Creator and representation of Him in the places He put them.

Jesus gives us a look at the heart and motivation of the Pharisees in Matthew 23. They were moved not by obedience to a relationship and the life-giving power of the God-breathed Scriptures but by the feel-good factor that comes from performing acts of apparent righteousness:

> The scribes and the Pharisees sit on Moses' seat, so do and observe whatever they tell you, but not the works they do. For they preach, but do not practice. They tie up heavy burdens, hard to bear, and lay them on people's shoulders, but they themselves are not willing to move them with their finger. They do all their deeds to be seen by others. (Matt. 23:2–5)

The Pharisees loved the feasts and being seen as truly religious people by all who attended: "They love the place of honor at feasts and the best seats in the synagogues and greetings in the marketplaces and being called rabbi by others" (Matt. 23:6–7). But they received their reward in being seen as righteous, since they lacked the circumcision of heart from which true righteousness must arise.

Jesus made possible a circumcised heart by planting the seed of the Father into those who are reconciled to Him, and He calls His followers to the genuine righteousness of God. Jesus told us that this righteousness comes from relationship to the Father through the Son: "Truly, truly, I say to you, whoever hears my word and believes him who sent me has eternal life. He does not come into judgment, but has passed from death to life" (John 5:24).

Jesus was clear about the fact that eternal life is not participation in a religion or its requirements but a restoration to the primary story of the Bible—that God is giving eternal relational and representative life to the sons of Adam who are found in the redeeming life and blood of His Son. As Jesus prayed shortly before He went to the cross, "This is eternal life, that they know you the only true God, and Jesus Christ whom you have sent" (John 17:3).

Genuine Righteousness in Relationships

The teaching model Jesus used in the Sermon on the Mount is, "The world thinks this way, but I say to you . . ." By means of contrast Jesus demonstrates throughout the rest of Matthew 5 just how different His righteousness is from that of this present world, both in the way it thinks and in the way it acts. In each example He gives, Jesus draws upon the original design of God as the most important principle and place to begin when it comes to how a child of God should live.

The righteousness of the Pharisees is in contrast to the righteousness that comes from the Father. While the theme of the Sermon on the Mount is righteousness, it speaks of a righteousness unlike that which can be produced by the seed of Adam. True righteousness must come from the seed of the last Adam, Jesus Christ, and is that which God designed from the beginning. It must be given to us through the salvation in the Son, worked into us by the Spirit, and acted on by us.

For example, the world sees murder as the worst treatment possible in human relations, but God's call to righteousness in interpersonal human relationships addresses the heart rather than the outward action:

> You have heard that it was said to those of old, "You shall not murder; and whoever murders will be liable to judgment." But I say to you that everyone who is angry with his brother will be liable to judgment; whoever insults his brother will be liable to the council; and whoever says, "You fool!" will be liable to the hell of fire. (Matt. 5:21–22)

Genuine righteousness is rooted in the creation of men and women in the image of God. People bear God's image, no matter how marred, and they are sustained in life by Him, even when they do not acknowledge it; thus they are to be treated with the dignity deserving of the divine image and as rightfully belonging to another. Our final accountability is to the One who made us: "Whoever sheds the blood of man, by man shall his blood be shed, for God made man in his own image" (Gen. 9:6).

Therefore anger, contempt, and disregard (calling someone a fool) are subject to judgment. This design of God is a pattern for Jesus' kingdom, and we are to be reconciled to God in these matters before we perform any religious observance. Look at pagan courts—even they settle quickly.

The comparative and contrastive statements in this portion of the Sermon on the Mount are powerful. But note this: Jesus' emphasis is not necessarily upon anger or disregard or contempt but upon the unchangeable design nature of God. God is love, and divine design calls us to love our neighbor. Because of our sin we will find ourselves from time to time out of relationship with people, but Ephesians 4:26 tells us that such out-of-relationship experiences should not be left unresolved beyond the same day they occur: "Do not let the sun go down on your anger." The Bible also indicates that there is a way for us to be angry and not sin: "Be angry, and do not sin; ponder in your own hearts on your beds, and be silent" (Ps. 4:4; see also Eph. 4:26).

The kingdom of God declared in the Sermon on the Mount by Jesus is built upon God's design for us in the beginning. Because of this, His children are to view other people as creations of God.

Relationships Are a Gift of God

That human beings have relationship with each other at all is a mark of God's righteous image within us. Left to our own desires and controlled by the self-serving nature within us, we would consume all relationships to our own benefit. Romans 3 gives us a glimpse into the depths of the human soul without the redeeming touch of the heavenly Father:

"None is righteous, no, not one; no one understands; no one seeks for God. All have turned aside; together they have become worthless; no one does good, not even one."
"Their throat is an open grave; they use their tongues to deceive."
"The venom of asps is under their lips."
"Their mouth is full of curses and bitterness."
"Their feet are swift to shed blood; in their paths are ruin and misery, and the way of peace they have not known."
"There is no fear of God before their eyes." (Rom. 3:10–18)

This is why James was so emphatic about the origin of tension between humans and their sometimes inflamed interactions:

Let no one say when he is tempted, "I am being tempted by God," for God cannot be tempted with evil, and he himself tempts no one. But each person is tempted when he is lured and enticed by his own desire. Then desire when it has conceived gives birth to

sin, and sin when it is fully grown brings forth death.
(Jas 1:13–15)

How great a forest is set ablaze by such a small fire! And the
tongue is a fire, a world of unrighteousness. The tongue is set
among our members, staining the whole body, setting on fire the
entire course of life, and set on fire by hell. For every kind of beast
and bird, of reptile and sea creature, can be tamed and has been
tamed by mankind, but no human being can tame the tongue. It
is a restless evil, full of deadly poison. (Jas 3:5–8)

Human relationships are from the design of God Himself, and as such, they are meant to be a blessing. This is why Jesus taught, "If you are offering your gift at the altar and there remember that your brother has something against you, leave your gift there before the altar and go. First be reconciled to your brother, and then come and offer your gift" (Matt. 5:23–24). We are to have regard for each other, even when conflict threatens to tear us apart.

In relationships we find the beauty of completeness in God creating Eve for Adam and Adam for Eve and giving them the ability to reproduce in kind, establishing the family. Created in the image of God and able to have relationship with Him, they were able to have relationship with each other. In this kind of relationship is the potential for the alleviation of loneliness, the celebration of companionship, and intimate dialogue. Sin has marred this original design, but in the rebirth of salvation in Jesus Christ, a fuller pursuit of relationship as well as all the other aspects of divine design is possible. Later, in eternity, we will have the unfettered experience of seeing the original design fully released from its marring of sin.

The Trinity itself interacts in harmonious relationship. The Holy Spirit who now lives within us speaks to us and disciplines us to walk increasingly in the divine design for human relationships. That is what Paul refers to when he talks about the fruit of the Spirit, or the fruit that the Spirit produces, in Galatians 5. Each fruit is a description of maturing interpersonal interactions with others and paints a picture of how God created relationship to be!

chapter 11

PURITY VS. LUST

As Jesus continues His sermon, He carries on with the contrasts between true and false righteousness in Matthew 5:27–32 with a discussion on purity in marriage and in gender relationships. The world sees adultery as the worst scenario in marriage, but Jesus says, "Everyone who looks at a woman with lustful intent has already committed adultery with her in his heart" (Matt. 5:28). "My call to marriage unions goes much deeper than what you see outwardly," Jesus is saying. "In fact, lust for another woman betrays My design. So control the eye, or get rid of it. Control your hand, or get rid of it" (see Matt. 5:29–30).

It is important for us to understand that Jesus was speaking to those who really wanted to be a part of His kingdom, to people who would be transformed by His coming death. They would be made new, and as new ones, they would become capable of saying no to the flesh.

Before we come to Jesus and are made new by His death, burial, and resurrection, we are dominated by the only alternative within us—our flesh. We noted from Romans 3 just how corrupt that flesh is. The sin nature is hostile to God and His designs, but when we are born again in Jesus Christ, God puts within us a new nature, one in which the Holy Spirit takes residence and one able to choose God's ways:

Are we to continue in sin that grace may abound? By no means! How can we who died to sin still live in it? Do you not know that all of us who have been baptized into Christ Jesus were baptized into his death? We were buried therefore with him by baptism into death, in order that, just as Christ was raised from the dead by the glory of the Father, we too might walk in newness of life. (Rom. 6:1–4)

God's Design for Purity and Commitment

This is the stark contrast that Jesus is making in the Sermon on the Mount. His kingdom is built upon both the original designs of God for the children of Adam and Eve and now more so upon the rebirth that comes through the death, burial, and resurrection of Jesus Christ, the Son of God. Because of this, the outward act of adultery betrays a deeper inward corruption, and before a person actually commits adultery, it begins in the consumptive, sinful look of adultery from the eye.

The apostle Paul, referring to the issue of sexual sin that begins in the heart and mind and then leads to action, wrote forcefully to the Thessalonians:

This is the will of God, your sanctification: that you abstain from sexual immorality; that each one of you know how to control his own body in holiness and honor, not in the passion of lust like the Gentiles who do not know God; that no one transgress and wrong his brother in this matter, because the Lord is an avenger in all these things, as we told you beforehand and solemnly warned you. For God has not called us for impurity, but in holiness. Therefore whoever disregards this, disregards not man but God, who gives his Holy Spirit to you. (1 Thess. 4:3–8)

Notice that this admonition is connected to the life and ministry of the Holy Spirit in us. When the Holy Spirit takes up residency in us as new believers, we become temples of the living God, as Paul says in 2 Corinthians 6:14–16, and therefore we are to have nothing to do with the ways of darkness:

> *Do not be unequally yoked with unbelievers. For what partnership has righteousness with lawlessness? Or what fellowship has light with darkness? What accord has Christ with Belial? Or what portion does a believer share with an unbeliever? What agreement has the temple of God with idols? For we are the temple of the living God; as God said, "I will make my dwelling among them and walk among them, and I will be their God, and they shall be my people."*

The Holy Spirit's ministry in us is to grow the seed of God that is now planted in us through our salvation in Jesus Christ. The purity that results from this will mature us to reject the sinful nature and instead be conformed to the image of Jesus and the original design of God.

Adultery is not only a breaking of the original design of how God intended men and women to relate, it is a corruption of the intimacy of the marriage relationship. C. S. Lewis explains it this way: "The monstrosity of sexual intercourse outside marriage is that those who indulge in it are trying to isolate one kind of union (the sexual) from all other kinds of unions which were intended to go along with it and make up the total union."[1] This is why Jesus went on to say that "everyone who divorces his wife, except on the ground of sexual immorality, makes her commit adultery, and whoever marries a divorced woman commits adultery" (Matt. 5:32).

God's original design for marriage is so strong that only adultery or death can break the union. Jesus also concludes that the strength of this union means that divorce for any reason results in adultery. These are strong words to the easy marriage-and-divorce patterns spreading in the world today. But they are not so much a "rule" that God puts into place about divorce, rather, they reflect the deep meaning in the design of marriage.

Marriage, as we saw in chapter 5 of this book, was birthed from the creative genius of God. The man and his wife are from the beginning intended to be partners in all that God has designed for His human creation to accomplish, a concept G. K. Chesterton expands on:

> It is quite clear that Christ believed in this sacrament [of marriage] in his own way and not in any current or contemporary way. He certainly did not get his argument against divorce from Mosaic law or Roman law or the habits of the Palestinian people. It would appear to his critics then exactly what it appears to his critics now: an arbitrary and transcendental dogma coming from nowhere save in the sense that it came from him.[2]

God's Design for Godly Marriage

In the garden God recognized Adam's aloneness, or, more explicitly, his incompleteness for God's created design of relationship to Him and representation of Him:

> *The Lord God said, "It is not good that the man should be alone; I will make him a helper fit for him." . . . So the Lord God caused a deep sleep to fall upon the man, and while he slept took one of his ribs and closed up its place with flesh. And the rib that the Lord God had taken from the man he made into a woman and brought her to the man. Then the man said, "This at last is bone of my bones and flesh of my flesh; she shall be called Woman, because she was taken out of Man." Therefore a man shall leave his father and his mother and hold fast to his wife, and they shall become one flesh. (Gen. 2:18–24)*

Both the man and the woman are intended for relationship with God. Each of them is to seek God through His Word and, in this epoch, through the indwelling Holy Spirit and in that daily seeking respond to God in obedience. This core relationship prepares each for greater meaning and unity in marriage and faithfulness in the family. Their united lives become an incarnation of the effects of transforming grace in and through them, both individually and together.

Out of the strength of their ongoing relationship with God, the husband and wife are to represent Him by stewarding the world He created for them to live in. God provided each of them with Spirit-given characteristics and gifts to use at times independently but coordinately and at other times in a unified effort. Some of this comes simply out of their relational obedience to Him and His Word as they live in their daily world—they show compassion, hospitality, and service to others as they invest their assets into the people around them. They also use their Spirit-given gifts to seek out ministry that Jesus gives to them.

The Bible describes some of the implications of this genius. In an almost mysterious way, the man and his wife become one. So in the beginning God says, "This is why a man leaves his father and mother and is united to his wife, and they become one flesh" (Gen. 2:24, NIV). God joined them together, and all man can do is bless and respect it. Jesus reiterates and expands this idea: "They are no longer two but one flesh. What therefore God has joined together, let not man separate" (Matt. 19:6).

The man and the woman are co-heirs of the life God intends for His people. With the accomplishment of Christ on the cross, Peter writes that a husband is to regard his wife "as heirs with [him] of the grace of life" (1 Pet. 3:7).

God judges those who do not respect the marriage vow: "The Lord is the witness between you and the wife of your youth. You have been unfaithful to her, though she is your partner, the wife of your marriage covenant" (Mal. 2:14, NIV).

Because of its design and intimacy, marriage is to be diligently protected. Hebrews 13:4 adds to the seriousness of the words of Malachi: "Marriage should be honored by all, and the marriage bed kept pure, for God will judge the adulterer and all the sexually immoral" (NIV).

God designed durability into the very nature of marriage. Paul, in addressing the durability of the marriage union, said, "A woman is bound to her husband as long as he lives. But if her husband dies, she is free to marry anyone she wishes" (1 Cor. 7:39, NIV). He added the admonition that if she does marry after the death of her husband, the new man must belong to the Lord.

Preserving and Pursuing Divine Design

God has designed the human experience to be one of mutual respect and working interdependency. Adultery, a sign of sexual thoughts and urges out of control, has significant negative impact upon this design. Most importantly, adultery destroys the deep, meaningful, purposed, and intimate relationship that God designed in the very beginning between a man and a woman in marriage.

The kingdom of Jesus, which we see expressed so eloquently in the Sermon on the Mount, is the incarnation of divine design. Those who follow Jesus realize the urgency of this design and seek to live it out. God's original design is so fundamental and urgent that the people of God will pursue it, cutting off anything that would risk their pursuit of it. With the fuller teaching of the New Testament to further illuminate the story of creation, we see that this urgency in us to pursue divine design is precisely the ministry of the Holy Spirit.

When we nurture our daily lives with the words of God in the Bible, we give the Holy Spirit God-breathed words of reminder, encouragement, rebuke and instruction to use in forming us in the life of Jesus and the image of God, both in our marriage relationships and in other aspects of life. We learn to say no to the rebellious urges of the flesh and yes to the designs of the new nature:

You must no longer walk as the Gentiles do, in the futility of their minds. They are darkened in their understanding, alienated from the life of God because of the ignorance that is in them, due to their hardness of heart. They have become callous and have given themselves up to sensuality, greedy to practice every kind of impurity. But that is not the way you learned Christ!—assuming that you have heard about him and were taught in him, as the truth is in Jesus, to put off your old self, which belongs to your former manner of life and is corrupt through deceitful desires, and to be renewed in the spirit of your minds, and to put on the new self, created after the likeness of God in true righteousness and holiness. (Eph. 4:17–24)

chapter 12

TRUTH AND LOVE VS. OATHS AND REVENGE

Continuing His contrasts between the people of God and those who adhere to the world's way of thinking or to a religious idea of righteousness, Jesus brings forth several final distinctions between the people of the kingdom and those of the world. We see these detailed in Matthew 5:33–48.

In these contrasts Jesus does not necessarily reveal to us everything that reflects the nature of the heavenly Father, but He tells us enough to show us two very important things: first, the ways in which the divine design transcends time and is to be reflected in every era of God's children—before the law, through the law, now in the fullness of Jesus, and one day in eternity—and second, the contrastive nature of the decisions and, therefore, the lives of His followers.

Do Not Take Oaths

Jesus begins with the matter of oaths: "You have heard that it was said to those of old, 'You shall not swear falsely, but shall perform to the Lord what you have sworn.' But I say to you, Do not take an oath at all" (Matt. 5:33–34).

The world thinks that an oath denotes a genuine and emphatic commitment. Sometimes an oath is a curse that makes an emphatic statement about another person, the strength of it confirming the feelings toward the other who has in some way offended or is simply disliked. Other times an oath is an assurance that purports to guarantee the strength of a promise or commitment made to another.

In either case, God did not give man that kind of authority. We do not have the right to decide the worth of another person or even to judge whether a person has pleased or disappointed us. As we will see later on in the Sermon on the Mount, Jesus commands us to act differently from the world, no matter what a person's provocation toward us:

> *If you forgive others their trespasses, your heavenly Father will also forgive you, but if you do not forgive others their trespasses, neither will your Father forgive your trespasses. (Matt. 6:14–15)*

> *Judge not, that you be not judged. For with the judgment you pronounce you will be judged, and with the measure you use it will be measured to you. Why do you see the speck that is in your brother's eye, but do not notice the log that is in your own eye? Or how can you say to your brother, "Let me take the speck out of your eye," when there is the log in your own eye? You hypocrite, first take the log out of your own eye, and then you will see clearly to take the speck out of your brother's eye. (Matt. 7:1–5)*

Created in the image of God, we have been given stewardship responsibility on this earth under His authority, but that authority does not extend beyond positive and active nurturing actions, toward both the world around us and the people who live in it, even when people act in ways that clearly display the marring of God's image. People belong to the Creator. He will decide their fate, and He will be their judge.

More so, as newborn ones in Jesus Christ, restored to the image of God, we are to act as Jesus Himself showed us by His life:

If there is any encouragement in Christ, any comfort from love, any participation in the Spirit, any affection and sympathy, complete my joy by being of the same mind, having the same love, being in full accord and of one mind. Do nothing from selfish ambition or conceit, but in humility count others more significant than yourselves. Let each of you look not only to his own interests, but also to the interests of others. Have this mind among yourselves, which is yours in Christ Jesus, who, though he was in the form of God, did not count equality with God a thing to be grasped, but emptied himself, by taking the form of a servant, being born in the likeness of men. And being found in human form, he humbled himself by becoming obedient to the point of death, even death on a cross. (Phil. 2:1–8)

The conclusion of these facts as they pertain to oaths is obvious, and Jesus states it in Matthew 5:34: don't swear at all! Not by heaven, because that is the abode of God, who rules it. Not by the earth, because we are merely stewards of this world, which belongs to God. Not by Jerusalem, for even though it is central in the Bible as a place of God's sovereignty, protection, and provision, no place can contain God's authority, and God has not given us some special right to claim it for ourselves (and in the world of eternity, the place of God and His Son will be the New Jerusalem, see Rev. 21:9–27). And not by our own head, for we "cannot make one hair white or black" (Matt. 5:36).

As representatives of God by His appointment, we are to steward the world around us simply and obediently. In Jesus man is now more capable of this kind of obedience than at any other time since Adam and Eve sinned and rejected God's terms for their representation, yet even so our present stewardship is limited in that neither we nor the earth are fully released from the curse in Adam and Eve and not yet citizens of the new heavens and earth. We have no unilateral authority over our stewardship in the world or even over our own bodies. We belong to another who has already set in motion who we are physically, emotionally, and intellectually.

> *You formed my inward parts; you knitted me together in my mother's womb. I praise you, for I am fearfully and wonderfully made. Wonderful are your works; my soul knows it very well. My frame was not hidden from you, when I was being made in secret, intricately woven in the depths of the earth. Your eyes saw my unformed substance; in your book were written, every one of them, the days that were formed for me, when as yet there was none of them. How precious to me are your thoughts, O God! How vast is the sum of them! If I would count them, they are more than the sand. I awake, and I am still with you. (Ps. 139:13–19)*

Even though at times we wonder at the results of this in people who have marred God's image and plan, God has His sovereign design in drawing all people to Himself:

> *[God] made from one man every nation of mankind to live on all the face of the earth, having determined allotted periods and the boundaries of their dwelling place, that they should seek God, and perhaps feel their way toward him and find him. Yet he is actually not far from each one of us, for "In him we live and move and have our being." (Acts 17:24–28)*

Because of our limited authority, our words must reflect the only power we actually possess: the power to say yes and no for today alone: "Let what you say be simply 'Yes' or 'No'; anything more than this comes from evil" (Matt. 5:37). We are to live daily in the sovereign designs, provision, and protection of our Father, who chooses to use us in His mercy agenda for the world.

The Believer's Response to Evil

Jesus lays forth His final contrasts between the children of God and the people of the world:

> *You have heard that it was said, "An eye for an eye and a tooth for a tooth." But I say to you, Do not resist the one who is evil. . . . You have heard that it was said, "You shall love your neighbor and hate your enemy." But I say to you, Love your enemies and pray for those who persecute you, so that you may be sons of your Father who is in heaven. (Matt. 5:38–45)*

The world considers revenge over a perceived or actual offense acceptable. But Jesus commands a different response: "God is able to deal with evil people in your life, so don't resist! Instead, offer the opposite—offer more: your cheek, your coat, your time, your effort. Like the model of your Lord and Savior, give, give, give!" (see Matt. 5:39–42).

Augustine expands on this thought:

Behold, O Lord our God, our Creator, when our affections have been restrained from love of the world, in which affections we were dying by living evilly, and when by living well a living soul has begun to exist, and your Word, by which you spoke to us through your apostle, has been fulfilled in us, namely, "Do not be conformed to this world," there follows what you immediately adjoined, and said, "But be reformed in the newness of your mind." No longer is this "after one's kind," as though imitating our neighbor who goes on before us or living according to the example of some better man. You did not say, "Let man be made according to his kind," but, "Let us make man to our image and likeness," so that we may prove what is your will.[1]

The world thinks that we should care for only those we know. But we are not to be like the world but like God, and He commands us to love our enemy—indeed, pray for our enemy! God's personal model, as we have seen, sets the highest standard: "Be perfect, as your heavenly Father is perfect" (Matt. 5:48). We must be children of the heavenly Father, for that is what we have been re-created to be. As John tells us,

> *Little children, let no one deceive you. Whoever practices righteousness is righteous, as he is righteous. Whoever makes a practice of sinning is of the devil, for the devil has been sinning from the beginning. The reason the Son of God appeared was to destroy the works of the devil. No one born of God makes a practice of sinning, for God's seed abides in him, and he cannot keep on sinning because he has been born of God. (1 John 3:7–9)*

God's goodness goes forth to the whole earth. Both the children of God and those people who remain in rebellion against Him receive a provision of His love. So we must love and greet all, even when—especially when—we have nothing personal to gain.

chapter 13

GIVING TO THE NEEDY

Jesus now changes His focus from contrasts to positive actions—things that we should do simply because we are children of God and members of the kingdom of Jesus. Each of these positive actions is introduced with the important admonition that they are not to be seen by others: "Beware of practicing your righteousness before other people in order to be seen by them, for then you will have no reward from your Father who is in heaven" (Matt. 6:1). Jesus begins in Matthew 6:1–4 by addressing the matter of giving to the needy.

These positive actions are not to be done to gain righteousness before God. God gives righteousness, or we never possess it: "If anyone is in Christ, he is a new creation. The old has passed away; behold, the new has come. All this is from God" (2 Cor. 5:17–18). Our positive actions are to be done in response to God Himself and therefore for God. He created us in Adam and Eve and re-created us in His Son, Jesus, to represent Him in this world, and therefore He calls us to accountability for the way in which we represent His image and likeness in us.

Indeed, even those who die without salvation in Jesus will be held accountable for how they represented God's image through their decisions and actions in this world:

I saw a great white throne and him who was seated on it. From his presence earth and sky fled away, and no place was found for them. And I saw the dead, great and small, standing before the throne, and books were opened. Then another book was opened, which is the book of life. And the dead were judged by what was written in the books, according to what they had done. And the sea gave up the dead who were in it, Death and Hades gave up the dead who were in them, and they were judged, each one of them, according to what they had done. Then Death and Hades were thrown into the lake of fire. This is the second death, the lake of fire. And if anyone's name was not found written in the book of life, he was thrown into the lake of fire. (Rev. 20:11–15)

Those of us who have been re-created in the image and likeness of the righteousness of our Creator through His death, burial, and resurrection are to live deliberately to represent that righteous likeness in the world, since "we are his workmanship, created in Christ Jesus for good works, which God prepared beforehand, that we should walk in them" (Eph. 2:10).

Because of our identification with Jesus, we are now able to give ourselves to righteousness instead of being slaves to all the decisions, rebellions, and actions of our former life without Him: "Thanks be to God, that you who were once slaves of sin have become obedient from the heart to the standard of teaching to which you were committed, and, having been set free from sin, have become slaves of righteousness" (Rom. 6:17–18).

These positive actions that Jesus explains here in Matthew 6 are to be done only because the Father has set His divine pattern in us and calls His children to live it out. If we do them for any other reason, we will receive no reward; we will receive our reward in performing our acts in front of others for our righteousness to be seen. Dietrich Bonhoeffer sheds insight on this truth:

Through God's own action in Christ we have been saved and not through our own works. We can never boast about them, for we are ourselves his workmanship. Yet it remains true that the whole purpose of our new creation in Christ is that in him we might attain unto good works. But all our good works are the works of God himself, the works for which he has prepared us beforehand. Good works then are ordained for the sake of salvation, but they are in the end those which God himself works within us. They are his gift, but it is our task to walk in them at every moment of our lives, knowing all the time that any good works of our own could never help us to abide before the judgment of God.[1]

Believers, like unbelievers, will have their actions in this world judged by God: "We make it our aim to please him. For we must all appear before the judgment seat of Christ, so that each one may receive what is due for what he has done in the body, whether good or evil" (2 Cor. 5:9–10). These actions have no impact on our righteousness in Jesus, for that was accomplished by the unilateral action of the Trinity: the Father deciding, the Son dying, and the Holy Spirit applying Christ's dying and resurrection to believers' lives. They do, however, impact our reward in heaven.

Giving Generously and Freely

The first positive action Jesus admonishes us to do with no observable fanfare is to give: "When you give to the needy, sound no trumpet before you, as the hypocrites do in the synagogues and in the streets, that they may be praised by others. Truly, I say to you, they have received their reward" (Matt. 6:2). If we give publicly, the recognition we receive for our action is all the reward we will get. Indeed, we are to give in such a way that our left hand is unaware of our right hand's action (see Matt. 6:3).

We are also to give with a measured disregard for our own preservation. The Father will care for our needs, as Jesus will show in the verses that follow. Since we are the expression of God's likeness and image in this world, He has designed that we meet the needs of others even as He has met our greatest need in His Son and continues to meet our daily needs.

Our giving should be so natural to us that we do not need to consult anyone, which we would typically do in other matters as interdependent members of the body of Christ. This is how our giving is to be done "in secret" (Matt. 6:4). If we live according to the Father's divine design, and the Spirit in us guides us specifically to give a certain person a certain amount, then we need know nothing more in order to act as our Father wants us to. The Father Himself rewards those who do as He designed (see Matt. 6:4)!

Paul adds further definition as to just how natural this giving ought to be for believers. Followers of Jesus are to "do good, to be rich in good works, to be generous and ready to share, thus storing up treasure for themselves as a good foundation for the future, so that they may take hold of that which is truly life" (1 Tim. 6:18–19).

God rejoices to give good gifts to us, His children. But since we are created in His image and likeness, the proper use of His gifts is the way in which He Himself used His riches: "For God so loved the world, that he gave his only Son, that whoever believes in him should not perish but have eternal life" (John 3:16). Jesus too is an example of the giving nature of God:

Have this mind among yourselves, which is yours in Christ Jesus, who, though he was in the form of God, did not count equality with God a thing to be grasped, but emptied himself, by taking the form of a servant, being born in the likeness of men. And being found in human form, he humbled himself by becoming obedient to the point of death, even death on a cross. (Phil. 2:5–8)

Paul recalls the words of Jesus, so simple yet so powerful: "It is more blessed to give than to receive" (Acts 20:35). Jesus was teaching us to live with our hands open! God gives us all things to enjoy (see 1 Tim. 6:17), but He wants us to understand that enjoyment for the child of God is found in following the example of the Father Himself. We are to be constantly sharing, giving away, and blessing others with the assets that God has placed in our hands to steward.

Old Testament Giving

Too many children of God begin the discussion of giving with the wrong point of view. They ask, "How much belongs to God?" or worse, "How much belongs to the church?" Even church leaders begin in the wrong place. Confusion abounds! Some believe that we are to give to the church, others to programs or missionaries; still others conclude that we are to give 10 percent. All of them site Malachi 3:10 completely out of context: "Bring the full tithe into the storehouse, that there may be food in my house. And thereby put me to the test, says the Lord of hosts, if I will not open the windows of heaven for you and pour down for you a blessing until there is no more need."

God did indeed prescribe an Old Testament pattern of giving for His people in the Mosaic law. First, God's people were to give as a result of their relationship to God, which was based on obedience to the law:

This is the commandment—the statutes and the rules—that the Lord your God commanded me to teach you, that you may do them in the land to which you are going over, to possess it, that you may fear the Lord your God, you and your son and your son's son, by keeping all his statutes and his commandments, which I command you, all the days of your life, and that your days may be long. (Deut. 6:1–2)

Second, they were to give a fixed portion of their total income as determined by God. For example,

Every tithe of the land, whether of the seed of the land or of the fruit of the trees, is the Lord's; it is holy to the Lord. If a man wishes to redeem some of his tithe, he shall add a fifth to it. And every tithe of herds and flocks, every tenth animal of all that pass under the herdsman's staff, shall be holy to the Lord. (Lev. 27:30–32)

Actually, when all the giving prescribed by the law was added up in all its differing forms, the portion that the people were to give of all that they produced was in excess of 30 percent.

Third, they were to give within the boundaries of the Mosaic law:

You shall tithe all the yield of your seed that comes from the field year by year. And before the Lord your God, in the place that he will choose, to make his name dwell there, you shall eat the tithe of your grain, of your wine, and of your oil, and the firstborn of your herd and flock, that you may learn to fear the Lord your God always. And if the way is too long for you, so that you are not able to carry the tithe, when the Lord your God blesses you, because the place is too far from you, which the Lord your God chooses, to set his name there, then you shall turn it into money and bind up the money in your hand and go to the place that the Lord your God chooses and spend the money for whatever you desire—oxen or sheep or wine or strong drink, whatever your appetite craves. And you shall eat there before the Lord your God and rejoice, you and your household. (Deut. 14:22–26)

New Testament Giving

The New Testament pattern of giving to the work of God, however, is quite distinct from that of the Old Testament. Giving to God in the

New Testament is a picture of our restoration to relationship and representation that we find in Adam and Eve and more fully in Jesus Christ.

First, we are to give, as those in the Old Testament were, as a result of our relationship to God, but in a relationship with God that is now personal. It is made possible through no one save Jesus Christ, our high priest (see Heb. 8:1–12). Because of His eternal high-priest representation for us in the very presence of God, we too are priests, represented in personal "face to face" relationship with God, as Peter so clearly states: "You yourselves like living stones are being built up as a spiritual house, to be a holy priesthood, to offer spiritual sacrifices acceptable to God through Jesus Christ" (1 Pet. 2:5).

Second, we are to give an unfixed portion of our total income as determined by the leading of the Holy Spirit within us. This is how we represent God, His nature, and His desires in our daily lives. We put all our assets each morning in our open hands and allow God to spend them as He wants. In doing this we take the admonition of Paul to heart:

Whoever sows sparingly will also reap sparingly, and whoever sows bountifully will also reap bountifully. Each one must give as he has decided in his heart, not reluctantly or under compulsion, for God loves a cheerful giver. And God is able to make all grace abound to you, so that having all sufficiency in all things at all times, you may abound in every good work. (2 Cor. 9:6–8)

Finally, we are to give according to grace, not the boundaries of the Mosaic law. New Testament believers were called to give for a variety of reasons: for the relief of other believers and the development of the church (see 2 Cor. 8–9) and the support of leaders and some elders (see 1 Cor. 9:14; Phil. 4:14–19).

Paul gives a clear pattern of New Testament giving in 1 Timothy 6:17–19. He first reminds believers not to be blinded by the world's point of view that wealth brings power: "Charge them not to be haughty, nor to set their hopes on the uncertainty of riches, but on God, who richly provides us with everything to enjoy" (1 Tim. 6:17). We don't deserve what we have, and to think that we do is arrogance. Our possessions won't take us any further than today, and we must not set our hopes on them. Instead, we are to hope in God, who is the giver of all that we enjoy. The fact is, as theologian Albert Barnes notes,

> The man who has not wealth may be vastly the superior of him who has; and for so slight and unimportant a distinction as gold can confer, no man should be proud. Besides, let such a man reflect that his property is the gift of God; that he is made rich because God has chosen to arrange things so that he should be; that it is not primarily owing to any skill or wisdom which he has; that his property only increases his responsibility.[2]

For the born again, true enjoyment is the opposite of what the world expects. We are to do good with our assets! Paul goes on to remind us that we should always look "to do good" and "to be rich in good works" by converting what we possess into something that helps another. We should "be generous," ready to give some of our resources away, and always "ready to share" all that we own (2 Tim. 6:18).

As children of another kingdom, re-created in the image of God, we will in this way store up "treasure for [ourselves] as a good foundation for the future, so that [we] may take hold of that which is truly life" (2 Tim. 6:19)—real life, as God designed it!

chapter 14

PRAYING AND FASTING

Another positive action that will characterize a child of God and one who is representing Him in this world is prayer, accompanied at times by fasting. Jesus addresses this matter in Matthew 6:5–18.

What exactly is prayer? Ideas about prayer formed by pagan rituals and practices have, to one degree or another, invaded Christian thinking and confused many. Pagan religions look at prayer as act of appeasement or petition, but the Christian has no need to appease God. The wrath of God has been fully appeased in the sacrifice of Jesus, the Son of God, so we need not fear approaching our Father through prayer:

Since, therefore, we have now been justified by [Christ's] blood, much more shall we be saved by him from the wrath of God. For if while we were enemies we were reconciled to God by the death of his Son, much more, now that we are reconciled, shall we be saved by his life. (Rom. 5:9–10)

There is no fear in love, but perfect love casts out fear. For fear has to do with punishment, and whoever fears has not been perfected in love. (1 John 4:18)

Equally, the Christian does not approach God only for petition. Pagan religions use petition as a means of obtaining what their adherents want, need, or feel they deserve. Christians do ask of God, but we do so from a selfless posture, and we never ask for what we believe we deserve—since what we deserve is judgment:

> The world is a stage for the exercise of mercy and judgment. It is not as if mankind were created by the hands of God, but as if they were God's enemies, granted by His grace enough light to return if they wish to seek and follow Him. Yet they also have enough light to receive punishment if they refuse to seek or to follow Him.[1]

But God has not given us judgment; instead, He has let our punishment fall upon His Son. Prayer for the child of God can never be separated from the relationship we now have with Him because of Jesus. When we ask of God, we ask because we have a relationship with Him and, because we are indwelt by His Holy Spirit, we ask according to God's directions and desires for us.

Prayer for the child of God is simply talking with God. Through prayer we build intimacy with the Lord as we listen to Him through His Word and respond in obedience to Him. Through prayer as our first order of business we acknowledge God's presence every morning: "The steadfast love of the Lord never ceases; his mercies never come to an end; they are new every morning; great is your faithfulness" (Lam. 3:22–23).

Through prayer and time in the Word, we regularly invite God into our day to invade our consciousness, and we then respond to what the Spirit says to us in the Word that day. This is the Spirit's job!

> *When the Spirit of truth comes, he will guide you into all the truth, for he will not speak on his own authority, but whatever he hears he will speak, and he will declare to you the things that are to come. He will glorify me, for he will take what is mine and declare it to you. (John 16:13–14)*

In God's presence we receive what we need for each day—forgiveness or repentance, rejoicing or correction, or receiving!

Examples of Prayer in Scriptures

In the chart below we see some instances of prayer in the Bible.

Passage	Idea	Application
Deuteronomy 4:7	Prayer that recognizes God's nearness to us	We must realize God's nearness to us when we pray (relationship to Him).
1 Samuel 12:19–25 (esp. 12:23)	Prayer for the people in their sin	The high priest stood in the gap for the nation (but his prayer did not preclude obedience in the people).
1 Samuel 1:9–27	Obedient and persistent prayer to have a son	We are to stand in the gap for our own needs.
2 Chronicles 7:11–22 (esp. 7:14)	Prayer with a promise and condition	God sovereignly chose Israel and would protect them if they asked and obeyed.
Job 42:8	Interceding to God for the sins of others	We are to stand in the gap for others, and God will forgive.
Psalm 122:6	Prayer for a city	We are to stand in the gap for Jerusalem.
Matthew 5:44	Prayer for those who persecute us	We are to stand in the gap for our enemies.
Luke 18:1	Praying and not giving up	Prayer is a "keep on asking" function.
Luke 22:40	Prayer in times of temptation	We are to stand in the gap for ourselves.
Romans 8:26	Prayer by the Holy Spirit for us	The Holy Spirit stands in the gap for us when we do not know what to ask for.
James 5:14–16	Prayer by the elders for the sick	The elders stand in the gap for others.

Prayer Must Be Genuine

Even though the people of God are to pray, Jesus warns us that prayer has its dangers:

> *When you pray, you must not be like the hypocrites. For they love to stand and pray in the synagogues and at the street corners, that they may be seen by others. Truly, I say to you, they have received their reward. But when you pray, go into your room and shut the door and pray to your Father who is in secret. And your Father who sees in secret will reward you. And when you pray, do not heap up empty phrases as the Gentiles do, for they think that they will be heard for their many words. Do not be like them, for your Father knows what you need before you ask him.*
> *(Matt. 6:5–8)*

When prayer is done only for the benefit of a watching public, it becomes hypocritical. We cannot seek relationship with God and at the same time "entertain" others with our spirituality in prayer.

Genuine prayer is intimate enough to be done in a closet. God meets His children in the most secret places when they pursue time alone with Him. In this kind of private prayer, we realize that God is listening to us. He always hears the true prayers of His children:

> *This is the confidence that we have toward him, that if we ask anything according to his will he hears us. And if we know that he hears us in whatever we ask, we know that we have the requests that we have asked of him. (1 John 5:14–15)*

> *The Lord is far from the wicked, but he hears the prayer of the righteous. (Prov. 15:29)*

> *The people of Israel groaned because of their slavery and cried out*

for help. Their cry for rescue from slavery came up to God. And God heard their groaning, and God remembered his covenant with Abraham, with Isaac, and with Jacob. God saw the people of Israel—and God knew. (Exod. 2:23–25)

True prayer begins with the knowledge that God already knows our need and has prepared a response for us according to His sovereign love.

When we desire a deeper time of listening to God, to His Word, and to the Holy Spirit, God often leads us to fast. This too is to be done without hypocrisy: "When you fast, anoint your head and wash your face, that your fasting may not be seen by others but by your Father who is in secret. And your Father who sees in secret will reward you" (Matt. 6:17–18). The world is used to hypocrites who fast to be seen. Those who do so have already gained their reward: being noticed by others!

Genuine fasting preserves a healthy countenance and a focus on the heavenly Father who has called us apart to be with Him. When we fast because God has called us apart to be in His presence and listen alertly to Him, we are rewarded by the heavenly Father.

Jesus' Model for Prayer

Jesus gives us a model for prayer, recorded in Matthew 6:9–15, in which we can see all the most important elements of talking with God. When we pray, Jesus instructs us to do a number of things:

- Acknowledge God's sovereignty: "Our Father in heaven"
- Bend to His sovereignty by setting apart His name: "Hallowed be your name"
- Prefer His kingdom: "Your kingdom come"
- Prefer His will: "Your will be done, on earth as it is in heaven"
- Acknowledge our need for God's daily provision: "Give us this

day our daily bread"
- Seek forgiveness as a daily course of action: "Forgive us our debts"
- Give forgiveness as a daily course of action: ". . . as we also have forgiven our debtors"
- Seek safety from temptation: "Lead us not into temptation"
- Seek safety from the evil one: "Deliver us from evil"

Jesus winds up by stating that forgiveness is the key to answered prayer, because it reflects the heart of our heavenly Father: "If you forgive others their trespasses, your heavenly Father will also forgive you, but if you do not forgive others their trespasses, neither will your Father forgive your trespasses" (Matt. 6:14–15).

Talking with God

In the divine design of God for His human creation, conversing with God as a part of our relationship with Him is natural and built upon many of the same aspects of discussion we have with people. God delights to have us converse with Him:

Some may say: It is not so much a question whether we are to pray by words or deeds as whether we are to pray at all if God already knows what is needful for us. Yet the very giving ourselves to prayer has the effect of soothing our minds and purifying them; it makes us more fit to receive the divine gifts which are spiritually poured out upon us.[2]

One important note: the emotional dynamic of our daily time with the heavenly Father will rise and fall with the seasons of life. When we are physically sick or especially busy in a needful task, our talking with God may need to take place as we go about our work.

Since talking with God should be a habit of our relationship with

Him, staying in touch with Him throughout the day is always possible; indeed, it is needful. When we start each day in His Word, giving our day and our very selves to the Spirit who lives within us, we are then ready to carry on an ongoing dialogue with the Father throughout the day. Then, when life affords us more controlled moments, we can spend deeper times of dialogue with God in silence, solitude, and fasting.

chapter 15

KEEPING OUR TREASURES IN HEAVEN

Jesus goes on to instruct His children in Matthew 6:19–34 in another positive action. He says, "Lay up for yourselves treasure in heaven, where neither moth nor rust destroys and where thieves do not break in and steal. For where your treasure is, there your heart will be also" (Matt. 6:20–21).

Our time on Earth is about God's mission, His kingdom, and our representation of Him in it. God wants us to put His kingdom first in our hearts, actions, and decisions and to trust Him with our earthly possessions and needs. In the transformed heart God has designed only one occupant: Himself. From this posture Matthew 6:19–34 is understandable, especially as a beginning point for stewarding our lives here on Earth in light of the transformation that begins with the new birth.

As we focus on God's mission in this world, we are not to worry about our earthly needs, as Jesus makes clear: "Therefore I tell you, do not be anxious about your life, what you will eat or what you will drink, nor about your body, what you will put on. Is not life more than food, and the body more than clothing?" (Matt. 6:25). If God takes care of the birds, the flowers of the field, and even the grass of the field, Jesus goes on, will He care for us any less? We can put God's kingdom first in our hearts and actions, and He will provide the rest for us: His kingdom and His righteousness.

Investing Our Wealth in Heaven

Why is Jesus so adamant about His children not storing up for themselves treasures on Earth? For six reasons that Jesus makes clear in this passage.

First, our treasures will rot in the bank of this world: "Do not lay up for yourselves treasures on earth, where moth and rust destroy and where thieves break in and steal" (Matt. 6:19). The world system wants us to think that we deserve our treasures, that they will finally make us truly happy, and that the better quality they are, the longer they will last because they are built to last! Jesus says just the opposite. Because our treasures are connected to this world and its passing nature, they will rot (see 1 John 2:17)—often even before we have an opportunity to use them. Sometimes they disappear because of the world's corrupt financial system in which they become opportunities for manipulative or cheating persons. Other times they disappear because someone openly steals them.

Second, eternity, designated for now as heaven, is the only true depository for our most cherished things—external wealth as well as internal things of life such as meaning, significance, and fulfillment: "Lay up for yourselves treasures in heaven, where neither moth nor rust destroys and where thieves do not break in and steal" (Matt. 6:20). God's bank is the most reliable place for us to deposit the things of our lives.

Third, whatever dominates our hearts owns us: "For where your treasure is, there your heart will be also" (Matt. 6:21). This is the clear message of the Bible. Treasures are not wrong in and of themselves; there is no sin inherent in created things. Sin lurks in the heart of men who want to create anything and everything to try to take the place of their Creator God—especially since their new gods are formed in their desired likeness and controlled by us!

Fourth, when our hearts are out of focus, our seeing ability is impaired: "The eye is the lamp of the body. So, if your eye is healthy, your whole body will be full of light, but if your eye is bad, your whole body will be full of darkness" (Matt. 6:22–23). The idea of living in darkness easily conjures up a picture of a host of demonic, manipulative, controlling, depressive ideas all common to the human experience. These come not from God's creative hand but from man's disobedient heart. The cumulative result of these things is a darkness that, if left to its own ends, leads to life on the raw side of ugly!

Fifth, in the world as God has created it, we must make a choice: either we are on the side of self and sin, or we are on the side of God and His redemption. As Jesus stated, "No one can serve two masters, for either he will hate the one and love the other, or he will be devoted to the one and despise the other. You cannot serve God and money" (Matt. 6:24). God, the Creator of this universe and therefore the One with the right to define its breadth, reasons, and limitations, has designed it so. One cannot serve two opposing forces.

God's new creation has only one occupant at its center: God Himself. Os Guinness explains it this way: "As the Bible reiterates, we become what we worship. Money almost literally seems to eat people away, drying up the sap of their vitality and withering their spontaneity, generosity, and joy."[1] He goes on to say,

> Money can assume an inordinate place in our lives until it becomes a personal, spiritual, god-like force that rules us— Mammon. Jesus' use of Mammon (Aramaic for "wealth") is unique—He gave it a strength and precision that the word never had before. He did not usually personify things, let alone deify them. And neither the Jews nor the nearby pagans knew a god by this name. But what Jesus says in speaking of Mammon is that money is a power—and not in a vague sense, as in the "force" of words. Rather, money is a power in the sense that it is an active agent with decisive spiritual power and is never

neutral. It is a power before we use it, not simply as we use it or whether we use it well or badly. As such, Mammon is a genuine rival to God.[2]

Finally, Jesus understood the potential for anxiety in living the kind of faith-filled life that God designed for His children, so He reminded us that God, if we are willing to trust Him, can take care of any anxiety: "Therefore I tell you, do not be anxious about your life, what you will eat or what you will drink, nor about your body, what you will put on. . . . But seek first the kingdom of God and his righteousness, and all these things will be added to you" (Matt. 6:25–33). God takes care of the birds and the flowers of the field, and He does so not with a minimum of care and attention but with lavish beauty. If He can care so expertly for these, He can care for our needs! Not only that, but He will do so not from a global posture of sweeping His hand over the whole of human need but personally, intimately—daily!

Paul's Thoughts on Laying Up Treasure in Heaven

The apostle Paul understood Jesus' command to store up our treasure in heaven and counseled Timothy accordingly, as we saw in chapter 13 of this book:

> Command those who are rich in this present world not to be ar-rogant nor to put their hope in wealth, which is so uncertain, but to put their hope in God, who richly provides us with everything for our enjoyment. Command them to do good, to be rich in good deeds, and to be generous and willing to share. In this way they will lay up treasure for themselves as a firm foundation for the coming age, so that they may take hold of the life that is truly life. (1 Tim. 6:17–19, NIV)

Echoing the words of Jesus, Paul commissioned Timothy to remind people of three things about worldly goods.

First, we are not to be arrogant regarding our possessions. Counter to what the world's system wants us to believe, we don't deserve worldly wealth, but arrogance comes easily to those who have great riches. "I have worked hard all my life . . ." a person begins, and one can almost hear the end of the thought, "so I deserve it." For the believer who does not take time to reflect and push back against the surrounding culture, arrogance can easily seep in.

Second, we must remember that the things we possess are not as solid as they appear to be or the system wants us to think they are, and thus we are not to put our hope in them. The world abounds with overt and subtle assumptions about the durability of what we possess. Thirty-year mortgage loans, lifetime warranties, new body parts, items that are "built to last" are all meant to seduce us into ignoring the obvious that nothing is built to last! Go ahead and use it, but don't put your hope in it!

Third, we must put our hope in God. Nothing can substitute for eternal hope. Perhaps the most damaging lie of the world regarding riches is that possessions can take the place of the God vacuum in the deepest recesses of a human life. What is it about substituting wealth for God that makes it so lethal?

What happened was this: People knew God perfectly well, but when they didn't treat him like God, refusing to worship him, they trivialized themselves into silliness and confusion so that there was neither sense nor direction left in their lives. They pretended to know it all, but were illiterate regarding life. They traded the glory of God who holds the whole world in his hands for cheap figurines you can buy at any roadside stand.

So God said, in effect, "If that's what you want, that's what you get." It wasn't long before they were living in a pigpen, smeared with filth, filthy inside and out. And all this because they traded

*the true God for a fake god, and worshiped the god they made
instead of the God who made them—the God we bless, the God
who blesses us. Oh, yes! (Rom. 1:21–25, MSG)*

How can we combat the pull of this worldview to pile up treasure
on Earth?

First, we must continually refocus our attention on God's divine
design of generosity for His children, reminding ourselves that this design is in antithesis and antagonism to the system we live in. Paul gives
us a picture of someone doing this in 1 Timothy 5:5: "The widow who
is really in need and left all alone puts her hope in God and continues
night and day to pray and to ask God for help" (NIV).

Second, we can combat the world's view by nurturing God's divine
design of giving that is in us:

*God is not unjust; he will not forget your work and the love you
have shown him as you have helped his people and continue to
help them. We want each of you to show this same diligence to the
very end, so that what you hope for may be fully realized. We do
not want you to become lazy, but to imitate those who through
faith and patience inherit what has been promised.*
(Heb. 6:10–12, NIV)

Third, we must embrace God's gifts and enjoy them, since God
"richly provides us with everything for our enjoyment" (1 Tim. 6:17,
NIV). Lest there be any doubt about what God means when He tells
us to enjoy good things, Paul immediately explained it to Timothy:
"Command them to do good" (1 Tim. 6:18, NIV). Earlier in 1 Timothy
Paul stated what is good in God's mind: "Have a reputation for helping
out with children, strangers, tired Christians, the hurt and troubled" (1
Tim. 5:10, MSG).

God makes a similar declaration to the people of Israel through the prophet Isaiah:

"If you get rid of unfair practices, quit blaming victims, quit gossiping about other people's sins, if you are generous with the hungry and start giving yourselves to the down-and-out, your lives will begin to glow in the darkness, your shadowed lives will be bathed in sunlight. I will always show you where to go. I'll give you a full life in the emptiest of places—firm muscles, strong bones. You'll be like a well-watered garden, a gurgling spring that never runs dry. You'll use the old rubble of past lives to build anew, rebuild the foundations from out of your past. You'll be known as those who can fix anything, restore old ruins, rebuild and renovate, make the community livable again.

"If you watch your step on the Sabbath and don't use my holy day for personal advantage, if you treat the Sabbath as a day of joy, God's holy day as a celebration, if you honor it by refusing 'business as usual,' making money, running here and there—then you'll be free to enjoy God! Oh, I'll make you ride high and soar above it all. I'll make you feast on the inheritance of your ancestor Jacob." Yes! God says so! (Isa. 58:9–14, MSG)

Why are these good things so important? Because they are the incarnated power of the new birth we have experienced in Jesus.

As Jesus said earlier in the Sermon on the Mount, "Now that I've put you there on a hilltop, on a light stand—shine! Keep an open house; be generous with your lives. By opening up to others, you'll prompt people to open up with God, this generous Father in heaven" (Matt. 5:16, MSG).

chapter 16

LETTING GOD BE THE JUDGE

In His list of positive actions that are part of God's divine design in the believer, Jesus includes refraining from judging others. Created in God's image and likeness, we are called to represent God by stewarding all He has given us in this world; that stewardship, however, has boundaries, and as children of God re-created in His image, we are not given authority to judge others. Jesus adds the logical expectation that if we judge others, we too will be judged and with the same measure we used to judge others. If we set ourselves up as judges, God will measure us by our own standard. We see all this expounded in Matthew 7:1–6:

> *Judge not, that you be not judged. For with the judgment you pronounce you will be judged, and with the measure you use it will be measured to you. Why do you see the speck that is in your brother's eye, but do not notice the log that is in your own eye? Or how can you say to your brother, "Let me take the speck out of your eye," when there is the log in your own eye? You hypocrite, first take the log out of your own eye, and then you will see clearly to take the speck out of your brother's eye. Do not give dogs what is holy, and do not throw your pearls before pigs, lest they trample them underfoot and turn to attack you.*

Jesus began, "Judge not, that you be not judged." The idea of judging here in the Sermon on the Mount is not so much about those within the body of Christ exhorting and correcting a brother in sin or one who is walking outside the best that God designed for him. Instead it has more to do with a judicial judgment about the worth of a person and the spirit from which this kind of judgment springs:

> The thing here condemned is that disposition to look unfavorably on the character and actions of others, which leads invariably to the pronouncing of rash, unjust, and unlovely judgments upon them. No doubt it is the judgments so pronounced which are here spoken of; but what our Lord aims at is the spirit out of which they spring.[1]

This does not mean that we are to have no input into other people's lives. But in order for us to speak effectively and rightly into men and women's lives, several things must take place first. First, we must work to accept people as God has made them, even when they have corrupted God's image. Second, we must be invited into the situation to give advice or correction. The invitation may come from the person himself or from the body of Christ taking loving corrective action toward the person, as Paul wrote about in Galatians 6:1–5. Finally, we have to be able to see ourselves clearly. Only when these three requirements have been met can we help someone else.

While we can move too harshly in judging others, we can also move too casually with others by giving what is holy to dogs or throwing precious stones to pigs (see Matt. 7:6). In other words, we are to use discernment when dispensing wisdom to others. If we do not, we ought not to be surprised when they trample the truth we give them and turn and attack us.

A person who does not accept God's Word often jests about it and mocks those who follow it. Peter warned the believers about such people:

Scoffers will come in the last days with scoffing, following their own sinful desires. They will say, "Where is the promise of his coming? For ever since the fathers fell asleep, all things are continuing as they were from the beginning of creation."
(2 Pet. 3:3–4)

But as Peter goes on to explain in the rest of 2 Peter 3 (which we will examine in chapter 18 of this book), those who scoff have missed much about what God has revealed, and they live under great deception.

God Will Be the Judge

The nature of fallen man is to think that we ourselves are always right, always better than the other person. But our vision is limited, distorted by the sin in our own eye. Only the righteous God is righteous and just and therefore able to see each man clearly. It is He who will hold each man and woman accountable to God.

But will God really judge people, even His own people? According to Hebrews He will:

If we go on sinning deliberately after receiving the knowledge of the truth, there no longer remains a sacrifice for sins, but a fearful expectation of judgment, and a fury of fire that will consume the adversaries. Anyone who has set aside the law of Moses dies without mercy on the evidence of two or three witnesses. How much worse punishment, do you think, will be deserved by the one who has trampled underfoot the Son of God, and has profaned the blood of the covenant by which he was sanctified, and has outraged the Spirit of grace? For we know him who said, "Vengeance is mine; I will repay." And again, "The Lord will judge his people." It is a fearful thing to fall into the hands of the living God. (Heb. 10:26–31)

The Lord will indeed judge men and women. He has promised this judgment for those who reject His gospel, His divine design, and it is a frightening thing.

But what about His own people—those of us who have been re-created in His image through the death, burial, and resurrection of Jesus Christ? Revelation 2 and 3 give a clear indication:

To the angel of the church in Ephesus write: . . . I know your works, your toil and your patient endurance. . . . Yet I have this against you, that you have abandoned the love you had at first. Remember therefore from where you have fallen; repent, and do the works you did at first. If not, I will come to you and remove your lampstand from its place, unless you repent. (Rev. 2:1–5)

To the angel of the church in Smyrna write: . . . I know your tribulation and your poverty. . . . Do not fear what you are about to suffer. . . . Be faithful unto death, and I will give you the crown of life. (Rev. 2:8–10)

To the angel of the church in Pergamum write: . . . You hold fast my name. . . . But I have a few things against you: you have some there who hold the teaching of Balaam. . . . Therefore repent. If not, I will come to you soon and war against them with the sword of my mouth. (Rev. 2:12–16)

To the angel of the church in Thyatira write: . . . I know your works, your love and faith and service and patient endurance. . . . But I have this against you, that you tolerate that woman Jezebel. . . . Those who commit adultery with her I will throw into great tribulation, unless they repent of her works, and I will strike her children dead. And all the churches will know that I am he who searches mind and heart, and I will give to each of you according to your works. (Rev. 2:18–23)

To the angel of the church in Sardis write: . . . I know your works. You have the reputation of being alive, but you are dead. Wake up, and strengthen what remains and is about to die, for I have not found your works complete in the sight of my God. (Rev. 3:1–2)

To the angel of the church in Philadelphia write: . . . I know your works. I have set before you an open door, which no one is able to shut. . . . Because you have kept my word about patient endurance, I will keep you from the hour of trial that is coming on the whole world, to try those who dwell on the earth. I am coming soon. Hold fast what you have. (Rev. 3:7–11)

To the angel of the church in Laodicea write: . . . You are neither cold nor hot. . . . So, because you are lukewarm, and neither hot nor cold, I will spit you out of my mouth. (Rev. 3:14–16)

Of the seven churches mentioned above, five were given notice of impending judgment, while two were not. While the churches in Ephesus, Pergamum, Thyatira, Sardis, and Laodicea received warnings to repent, the church in Smyrna was told that if they remained faithful while the devil tested them, they would receive "the crown of life" (Rev. 2:10), and the church in Philadelphia was told by God, "I will keep you" (Rev. 3:10).

In Revelation 2 and 3 we see principles to learn and live by in light of God's coming judgment of His people. First, God says to every body of believers, "He who has an ear, let him hear" (see Rev. 2:7, 11, 17, 29; 3:6, 13, 22). To those Christians who overcome sin and temptation, God gives ability to eternity (see Rev. 2:7), resilience to eternity (see Rev. 2:11), identity in eternity (see Rev. 2:17), position, purpose, and place in eternity (see Rev. 2:26–28), permanency in eternity (see Rev. 3:5), ownership in eternity (see Rev. 3:11), and royalty in eternity (see Rev. 3:21).

Second, those whom God loves He rebukes (see Rev. 3:19, 2:6, 16, 23; 3:3, 16). Some believers might say, "What do we need to repent of?" We need to repent of having forsaken our first love (see Rev. 2:4), harboring heresy (see Rev. 2:14–15, 20), being dead (see Rev. 3:1), and thinking we are godly when we are not (see Rev. 3:17).

Finally, if we are children of God, we do not need to be afraid of what we may suffer (see Rev. 2:10); instead, we are to be faithful to God, even to the point of death (see Rev. 2:10). We must hold on (see Rev. 2:25) to the light we possess and not go back in our growth (see Rev. 3:11) so that we won't lose our crown to anyone trying to take it from us. We are to remember and obey (see Rev. 3:3) what we have heard and received and live up to the light we possess.

A final word on the judgment of God: if we persist in living according to God's divine design for the believer, we will receive a reward! "Do not throw away your confidence, which has a great reward. For you have need of endurance, so that when you have done the will of God you may receive what is promised" (Heb. 10:35–36).

chapter 17

SEEKING GOD AND LOVING OTHERS

As Jesus nears the end of His Sermon on the Mount and His description of divine design in the believer, He gives several spiritual disciplines for the people of God to live by. We see three of those here in Matthew 7:7–14: seeking God in prayer, treating others as we would wish to be treated, and choosing the narrow road that leads to life.

Seeking God

First, as children of God re-created in His image, we are called to be diligent seekers of God: "Ask, and it will be given to you; seek, and you will find; knock, and it will be opened to you. For everyone who asks receives, and the one who seeks finds, and to the one who knocks it will be opened" (Matt. 7:7–8). God provides His presence and direction to those who build a lifestyle of seeking. The asker receives; the seeker finds; to the knocker the door is opened. All these reinforce a thought running throughout Scripture: God not only hears our petitions—He answers them.

These promises are connected to the greater context of the Sermon on the Mount: as we pursue the design of God for believers in His Son, Jesus, through the residency in us of His Holy Spirit, we will receive answers to the questions we ask, provision as we seek deeper relationship with God and representation of Him, and direction in the way of open doors. As we walk this new life of seeking that God designed for us from the very beginning, we will come up against doubts, questions, and weaknesses, but for each of them there is an answer, because God the Spirit is active on our behalf:

> *We do not know what to pray for as we ought, but the Spirit himself intercedes for us with groanings too deep for words. And he who searches hearts knows what is the mind of the Spirit, because the Spirit intercedes for the saints according to the will of God. (Rom. 8:26–27)*

God has prepared a path for each of His children to walk, and as we travel that path, He expects us to turn to Him for the direction in our difficulties and find His provision. In the Gospel of John alone, we find many promises for God's provision:

> *Whatever you ask from God, God will give you. (John 11:22)*

> *Whatever you ask in my name, this I will do, that the Father may be glorified in the Son. (John 14:13)*

> *If you ask me anything in my name, I will do it. (John 14:14)*

> *If you abide in me, and my words abide in you, ask whatever you wish, and it will be done for you. (John 15:7)*

> *In that day you will ask nothing of me. Truly, truly, I say to you, whatever you ask of the Father in my name, he will give it to you. (John 16:23)*

> *Until now you have asked nothing in my name. Ask, and you will receive, that your joy may be full. (John 16:24)*

Of course, in each of these passages in which God promises supply is the condition that the requests come from His true children—those who have been restored to Him through salvation in Jesus Christ. Only the children of God can ask the right things, because we have come to realize that we are created by God and for God to represent Him and His mercy ministry across time, and we learn to ask in connection to our calling and mission for Him. This does not mean that we will not occasionally ask for the wrong thing, but when we do, we are submissive to God's loving sovereignty as it specifically applies to our lives. We trust His judgment, and therefore we trust His provision!

Imagine, if we give good gifts to those we love, how much more will our "Father who is in heaven give good things to those who ask him!" (Matt. 7:11).

Living a Life of Love

Second, as we pursue life as God has designed and as Jesus described in the Sermon on the Mount, we are called to live a life of love: "Whatever you wish that others would do to you, do also to them, for this is the Law and the Prophets" (Matt. 7:12). Jesus Himself is the model for this life of love:

Jesus called [His disciples] to him and said, "You know that the rulers of the Gentiles lord it over them, and their great ones exercise authority over them. It shall not be so among you. But whoever would be great among you must be your servant, and whoever would be first among you must be your slave, even as the Son of Man came not to be served but to serve, and to give his life as a ransom for many." (Matt. 20:25–28)

The disciples learned this lesson directly from Jesus. When they fought on one occasion over position and authority, Jesus made clear, "It shall not be so among you." Instead, they were to live as He was living, giving Himself for others. Jesus lived the law of love!

> *This is the message that you have heard from the beginning, that we should love one another. We should not be like Cain, who was of the evil one and murdered his brother. And why did he murder him? Because his own deeds were evil and his brother's righteous. Do not be surprised, brothers, that the world hates you. We know that we have passed out of death into life, because we love the brothers. Whoever does not love abides in death. Everyone who hates his brother is a murderer, and you know that no murderer has eternal life abiding in him. By this we know love, that he laid down his life for us, and we ought to lay down our lives for the brothers. (1 John 3:11–16)*

Choosing the Narrow Road

Third, as we follow this life of love in obedience to the commandments of Jesus, we will be consistently called upon to stay on the least favored road: "Enter by the narrow gate. For the gate is wide and the way is easy that leads to destruction, and those who enter by it are many. For the gate is narrow and the way is hard that leads to life, and those who find it are few" (Matt. 7:13–14). The road to destruction is wide and heavily populated, while the one to life is narrow and can be lonely. But this is the path Jesus walked, and it is the path that God's children must take as well.

We must guard against becoming lazy about pursuing God's design for our lives as we seek to grow in relationship with Him and represent Him in this world. Instead, Hebrews 10 tells us, "Let us consider how to stir up one another to love and good works, not neglecting to meet together, as is the habit of some, but encouraging one another, and all the more as you see the Day drawing near" (Heb. 10:24–25). Oswald Chambers offers some insight on choosing the narrow path:

We are all capable of being spiritually lazy saints. We want to stay off the rough roads of life, and our primary objective is to secure a peaceful retreat from the world. The ideas put forth in these verses from Hebrews 10 are those of stirring up one another and of keeping ourselves together. Both of these require initiative—our willingness to take the first step toward Christ-realization, not the initiative toward self-realization. To live a distant, withdrawn, and secluded life is diametrically opposed to spirituality as Jesus Christ taught it.

The true test of our spirituality occurs when we come up against injustice, degradation, ingratitude, and turmoil, all of which have the tendency to make us spiritually lazy. While being tested, we want to use prayer and Bible reading for the purpose of finding a quiet retreat. We use God only for the sake of getting peace and joy. We seek only our enjoyment of Jesus Christ, not a true realization of Him. This is the first step in the wrong direction. All these things we are seeking are simply effects, and yet we try to make them causes.

"Yes, I think it is right," Peter said, "to stir you up by reminding you" (2 Peter 1:13). It is a most disturbing thing to be hit squarely in the stomach by someone being used of God to stir us up—someone who is full of spiritual activity. Simple active work and spiritual activity are not the same thing. Active work can actually be the counterfeit of spiritual activity. The real danger in spiritual laziness is that we do not want to be stirred up—all we want to hear about is a spiritual retirement from the world. Yet Jesus Christ never encourages the idea of retirement—He says, "Go and tell My brethren" (Matthew 28:10).[1]

Such active discipline and determination are required if we are going to remain on the narrow path that Jesus calls believers to.

The Joy of the Spiritual Disciplines

God invites believers in Christ to ask, seek, and knock. He always hears our petitions and answers them, bestowing good gifts on His children. God also invites us to treat those around us just as we would want to be treated, living a life of love, as Jesus did, in a dark world. Most importantly, He invites us daily to enter the mystery of life as He designed it and abandon ourselves to Him, choosing the narrow when so many others will not. When we do, the result will be as it was for the psalmist: "He put a new song in my mouth, a song of praise to our God. Many will see and fear, and put their trust in the Lord" (Ps. 40:3).

chapter 18

WATCHING OUT FOR DECEPTION

Having given a partial but concise depiction of divine design in the life of the believer in His Sermon on the Mount, Jesus now gives His final charge to the Christian in the way of a warning. Those of us who have been re-created in the image and likeness of God must guard against deception, and we must protect ourselves from destruction by building our lives on the foundation of God's Word and practicing what it says.

Discerning Deception

The New Testament is filled with warnings about deception and being deceived. We are warned often to stay alert to people outside the church who want to subvert the faith. But we are also warned about people inside the church parading as believers who want to prey upon the faithful for personal gain.

Jesus warns us to watch out for deception from people posing as religious leaders: "Beware of false prophets, who come to you in sheep's clothing but inwardly are ravenous wolves. You will recognize them by their fruits" (Matt. 7:15–16). The aim of such individuals is to destroy. With time and observation on our part, however, the fruit of their lives will reveal what is really inside them, despite the confessions they make with their mouths. When we pick fruit from grape vines and fig trees, we expect to reap grapes and figs, not thorns or thistles.

Jesus also warns us to watch for deception from people posing as true followers of God, and He gives us a guaranteed way to recognize them: "Not everyone who says to me, 'Lord, Lord,' will enter the kingdom of heaven, but the one who does the will of my Father who is in heaven" (Matt. 7:21). We are to look for those who do God's will—those who demonstrate that they know God by their relationship with Him and their representation of Him in the world around them.

If it were easy to recognize these people and their errors, there would be no need for warning or a history of heresy in every generation of the church since Jesus went to be with the Father. One of the things that makes recognizing deception difficult in our day is that so many have easy access into our lives through the Internet, radio, and TV. The use of these forms of media is not necessarily wrong, but because we are not able to see the daily lives of the ones communicating to us through them, we must be extra careful about what we take from these teachers.

The best way to protect ourselves from error is twofold. One, as we have noted often throughout this book, we must spend time every day in God's Word, growing in the grace and knowledge that has come to us through our Lord Jesus Christ, the prophets of old, and the apostles. The Word is God breathed and able therefore to nurture us in God's divine design for us. As we read the Word, we also need the Holy Spirit who lives within us to instruct us in God's truth. "The Helper, the Holy Spirit, whom the Father will send in my name, he will teach you all things and bring to your remembrance all that I have said to you" (John 14:26). The apostle Paul adds, "Follow the pattern of the sound words that you have heard from me, in the faith and love that are in Christ Jesus. By the Holy Spirit who dwells within us, guard the good deposit entrusted to you" (2 Tim. 1:13–14). The Holy Spirit is always within us to help us guard the things that we have learned from the prophets and apostles to whom was commended the writing of the words of God and to mature in us the life of God's Son.

Second, we must look to the leaders who shepherd our local congregation for the majority of our spiritual learning. While they may not always be the most theologically qualified teachers or even the most interesting, yet we can test what they say against what they do in their lives. We can watch our leaders' lives and see how they measure up to the many kingdom descriptions that Jesus has given to us here in the Sermon on the Mount. We must recognize, of course, that no one is perfect, but we can ask of our leaders, are they maturing in these things?

Maturation in the things of God is proof of time spent daily in God's Word and the resident work of the Holy Spirit:

Those who live according to the flesh set their minds on the things of the flesh, but those who live according to the Spirit set their minds on the things of the Spirit. For to set the mind on the flesh is death, but to set the mind on the Spirit is life and peace. For the mind that is set on the flesh is hostile to God, for it does not submit to God's law; indeed, it cannot. Those who are in the flesh cannot please God.

You, however, are not in the flesh but in the Spirit, if in fact the Spirit of God dwells in you. Anyone who does not have the Spirit of Christ does not belong to him. But if Christ is in you, although the body is dead because of sin, the Spirit is life because of righteousness. If the Spirit of him who raised Jesus from the dead dwells in you, he who raised Christ Jesus from the dead will also give life to your mortal bodies through his Spirit who dwells in you. (Rom. 8:5–11)

When we cannot see in a spiritual teacher's daily life the godly qualities that are naturally nurtured by the Word of God and ministered by the Spirit of God in the midst of the people of God, we need to be cautious. Eternity will surprise us as to who knew God and who did not: "On that day many will say to me, 'Lord, Lord, did we not prophesy in your name, and cast out demons in your name, and do many mighty works in your name?' And then will I declare to them, 'I never knew you; depart from me, you workers of lawlessness'" (Matt. 7:22–23).

Scoffers Miss the Truth Because They Scorn God's Word

The world is full of religious people, both leaders and followers, who act as if they are genuine. But the true follower of Jesus has the seed of God within him and the Spirit of God to grow it, and therefore he will progressively look more and more like the Son, Jesus Christ. Look at the person's fruit! Sadly, many who do the work of God do not know God, and we know this because their personal fruit shows that they are not growing to look like Jesus Christ.

The second chapter of 2 Peter gives an account of the inner lives of people who are within the church but only seek to deceive and profit from it. The final words of that chapter are some of the most graphic in the Bible:

> *These are waterless springs and mists driven by a storm. For them the gloom of utter darkness has been reserved. For, speaking loud boasts of folly, they entice by sensual passions of the flesh those who are barely escaping from those who live in error. They promise them freedom, but they themselves are slaves of corruption. For whatever overcomes a person, to that he is enslaved. For if, after they have escaped the defilements of the world through the knowledge of our Lord and Savior Jesus Christ, they are again entangled in them and overcome, the last state has become worse for them than the first. For it would have been better for them never to have known the way of righteousness than after knowing it to turn back from the holy commandment delivered to them. What the true proverb says has happened to them: "The dog re-*

turns to its own vomit, and the sow, after washing herself, returns to wallow in the mire." (2 Pet. 2:17–22)

Peter gives us the primary antidote to being deceived in 2 Peter 3. As believers, we are to consistently "remember the predictions of the holy prophets" (2 Pet. 3:2), noting the prophecies that have been fulfilled, those that are being fulfilled, and those yet to be fulfilled. Further, we must meditate on and obey the commandments of our Lord and Savior, Jesus Christ. These evil people in our midst parading around like followers of Jesus are a danger to the believer who is not watching and growing. Peter describes them and warns us, reminding us that God's antidote is in His Word.

Peter goes on in 2 Peter 3, in his last recorded words to the church, to talk about the danger from those outside the church as well:

Scoffers will come in the last days with scoffing, following their own sinful desires. They will say, "Where is the promise of his coming? For ever since the fathers fell asleep, all things are continuing as they were from the beginning of creation."
(2 Pet. 3:3–4)

Those who are not followers of Jesus do not view our convictions about the Word of God, its divine origin, or its God-inspired power as we do. Therefore, we should not be surprised at their reactions to our convictions, life decisions, and expectations. Scoffers will question God's truth in the final days. These scoffers will be moved by their own sinful desires and will have a backward view of history without God! When they look back down the corridor of history without the lens of Scripture, they cannot see anything different from what their fathers believed or practiced.

But don't worry—they have ignored four things!

First, they ignore the fact that God made the world and put a witness of accountability and judgment in it: "They deliberately overlook this fact, that the heavens existed long ago, and the earth was formed out of water and through water by the word of God, and that by means of these the world that then existed was deluged with water and perished" (2 Pet. 3:5–6). The story of Noah reminds us that God who made the world has a right to judge it, and He can do so. Now with the completed Bible in our hands, we know that He will. In the future judgment, as He promised Noah, He will not flood the earth and rescue only a few out of it to repopulate it; instead He will destroy it all, taking out of it to Himself those who belong to Him, who are washed by the blood of His Son, Jesus Christ.

Second, they fail to recognize that God has the world held under judgment, waiting for a day of destruction. The fact that He has not yet judged the world does not mean that He will not do so. Instead, "by the same word the heavens and earth that now exist are stored up for fire, being kept until the day of judgment and destruction of the ungodly" (2 Pet. 3:7).

Third, they fail to recognize that God is not in a hurry, because something else besides judgment is moving Him: the story of history. "Do not overlook this one fact, beloved, that with the Lord one day is as a thousand years, and a thousand years as one day" (2 Pet. 3:8).

Fourth, they fail to recognize that mercy is moving history! "The Lord is not slow to fulfill his promise as some count slowness, but is patient toward you, not wishing that any should perish, but that all should reach repentance" (2 Pet. 3:9). As Peter wrote, we are to "count the patience of our Lord as salvation" (2 Pet. 3:15).

The promised day of judgment will come, as we saw clearly in chapter 16 of this book, and when it does, it will come like a thief, unannounced. It will be instantaneous, like an arrow shot toward its mark, and it will come with a roar! It will be intense, like the heat of a fever! It will be complete—the very molecules will come undone! "The day of the Lord will come like a thief, and then the heavens will pass away with a roar, and the heavenly bodies will be burned up and dissolved, and the earth and the works that are done on it will be exposed" (2 Pet. 3:10).

Since we know the end of the story, "what sort of people ought [we] to be?" (2 Pet. 3:11). We are to be holy, set apart, godly (see 2 Pet. 3:12), even while others deceive and are deceived. We are to act like God's children, anticipating that day and advancing its coming by carrying out our role in representation of God on Earth: expanding His kingdom through extending the gospel message!

Build Wisely

Jesus concludes His warning and His sermon with the admonition to build wisely:

Everyone then who hears these words of mine and does them will be like a wise man who built his house on the rock. And the rain fell, and the floods came, and the winds blew and beat on that house, but it did not fall, because it had been founded on the rock. And everyone who hears these words of mine and does not do them will be like a foolish man who built his house on the sand. And the rain fell, and the floods came, and the winds blew and beat against that house, and it fell, and great was the fall of it. (Matt. 7:24–27)

For those of us who have been re-created in God's image, the best protection we have against deception is to hear the words of Jesus and put them into practice. When we listen intently to the commands of God as expressed in His Word and then live out the picture presented to us in the Sermon on the Mount, we will be protected when the storms of sin and deception swirl around us.

This brings us back once again to relationship and representation—we must nurture our relationship with God through time with Him in His Word, which will lead to maturity, holiness, and service for Him in this world. Commenting on the importance of daily time in God's Word as a protection against the deification of human reasoning,

C. H. Mackintosh wrote, "Under the dominion of rationalism the soul is like a vessel broken from its safe moorings in the haven of divine revelation, to be tossed like a cork upon the wild watery waste of universal skepticism."[1] The life that is built upon deceptive human reasoning has no foundation in the Word and will collapse!

God intends His Word to not only instruct but to transform: "Do not be conformed to this world, but be transformed by the renewal of your mind" (Rom. 12:2). Transformation takes place as we do the things we discussed in chapter 3 of this book: prioritize Scripture on a daily basis and embrace the healing ministry of the Word and of our high priest (see Heb. 4:12–16) as we build the relational disciplines of silence, solitude, and submission.

chapter 19

LIVING IN ORDER TO PLEASE GOD

God's divine design is life! In the very beginning God breathed His own life into us: "The Lord God formed the man of dust from the ground and breathed into his nostrils the breath of life, and the man became a living creature" (Gen. 2:7). This life of God, re-created in believers in the image of Christ, is exactly what Jesus sought to define for us in the Sermon on the Mount.

William Wilberforce, of abolition fame, wrote of the effect that this life of God should have in us:

> True faith is something that so pervades our lives that it affects everything we do. It is a matter of the heart, where its reality becomes our supreme influence. It seeks to root out anything that is contrary to its truth and attempts to bring all of the heart's desires and affection under its control.[1]

The Mosaic covenant was intended to give life as lived within the boundaries of God's design and provision:

> *My covenant with [Levi] was one of life and peace. (Mal. 2:5)*

> *Where sin increased, grace abounded all the more, so that, as*
> *sin reigned in death, grace also might reign through righteous-*
> *ness leading to eternal life through Jesus Christ our Lord. (Rom.*
> *5:20–21)*

This life God gave us was intended to be lived in a world with no sin. Adam and Eve's rebellious choice to disobey God ruined that possibility here on Earth, but a sinless world will come when God's agenda of mercy is finally accomplished on this earth:

> *The Lord is not slow to fulfill his promise as some count slowness,*
> *but is patient toward you, not wishing that any should perish,*
> *but that all should reach repentance. But the day of the Lord will*
> *come like a thief, and then the heavens will pass away with a*
> *roar, and the heavenly bodies will be burned up and dissolved,*
> *and the earth and the works that are done on it will be exposed.*
> *(2 Pet. 3:9–10)*

In the meantime, though, we are still called to life, and we find it in deep relationship with God and representation of Him in this world.

Who We Are and Why We Exist

As this book has attempted to explain, this dual calling answers two of the deepest questions in the heart of man: who am I? and, why do I exist? For the believer in Jesus Christ, relationship with God and representation of Him define the rest of life on this earth.

From the original creation in Adam and Eve, we learned who we are: we are created by God the Father for God the Father. But because of the sin we were born into and the rebellious actions we have done, we were alienated from God, and we lost the joy and beauty of that God-created purpose.

That kind of me-centered thinking has brought about catastrophic results in everything we touch. Our marriages are marred with the effects of abuse, infidelity, and brokenness. Our children ignore their parents and, ultimately, any and all authority as they pursue life on their own terms. Our societies and the institutions within them are corrupted with oppression, abuse, greed, and power mongering. The words of God in Romans 3 aptly describe the essence of man without God:

> *"None is righteous, no, not one; no one understands; no one seeks for God. All have turned aside; together they have become worthless; no one does good, not even one."*
> *"Their throat is an open grave; they use their tongues to deceive."*
> *"The venom of asps is under their lips."*
> *"Their mouth is full of curses and bitterness."*
> *"Their feet are swift to shed blood; in their paths are ruin and misery, and the way of peace they have not known."*
> *"There is no fear of God before their eyes." (Rom. 3:10–18)*

But in Jesus Christ, as we have seen, God has restored His original intentions for those who have come to Him for salvation. In the death, burial, and resurrection of His Son, our Savior, Jesus Christ, we are reconnected to the God-defined essence of who we are meant to be in the image and likeness of God.

Further, in that original creation we were given the answer to why we exist: "The Lord God took the man and put him in the garden of Eden to work it and keep it" (Gen. 2:15). We were created to represent God on the planet He made for us.

Who are we? We are creations of God Himself, made in His image and likeness. Why do we exist? We exist to represent Him wherever He takes us in this life. Indeed, we will spend eternity fulfilling both of these original designs of God in a world without sin.

Planning to Please God

So we were created and re-created for life, even in this fallen world, in this era of mercy. Because of this divine design, how we order our lives is important. For those of us who have been transformed by our identification with Jesus in His death, burial, and resurrection, we are to live in a way that pleases God.

Paul gives us some direction as to how to do this, as we see in his words to the Thessalonians: "We instructed you how to live in order to please God, as in fact you are living. Now we ask you and urge you in the Lord Jesus to do this more and more" (1 Thess. 4:1, NIV).

First, Paul calls the Thessalonians to be sanctified: "This is the will of God, your sanctification" (1 Thess. 4:3). Sanctification consists of two things: ceasing to do evil and learning to do well. The first work of maturing into the righteousness that God designed and that is seen in the life of Jesus is to say no to the propensities toward evil in our flesh. We must recognize, check, and subdue the unrighteous habits that we formed before we became followers of Jesus Christ. The second part of the work consists in learning to act on what God the Spirit is teaching us and living out the incarnational aspects of being His follower.

Second, we must "abstain from sexual immorality" (1 Thess. 4:3). The word for "sexuality immorality" in the original language is *porneia* (πορνεια). It refers to uncleanness of any kind. We must plan to keep our hearts and minds free of images and thoughts that play into the hand of this world's obsessions. The apostle John put it this way:

Do not love the world or the things in the world. If anyone loves the world, the love of the Father is not in him. For all that is in the world—the desires of the flesh and the desires of the eyes and pride of life—is not from the Father but is from the world. And the world is passing away along with its desires, but whoever does the will of God abides forever. (1 John 2:15–17)

The desires of the flesh (the lusts that come from our sinful nature), the desires of the eyes (those things that are so pleasing to our vision), and the pride of life (the things that make us feel important, worthwhile, and significant) are all opposed to the way in which God designed those created in His image and likeness to live. They are cheap substitutes!

Third, we must know our bodies and control them "in holiness and honor, not in the passion of lust like the Gentiles who do not know God" (1 Thess. 4:4–5). We are not to act like the world, defrauding our brother of that which belongs to him when it comes to sexual matters. The world is rife with people who steal what does not belong to them, breaking into houses and cars and carrying away what they did not work to buy, but in this case Paul is referring to stealing another man's wife—the sin of adultery.

Living the Life of Christ Requires Discipline

If we are to embrace what God intended us to have and that Jesus spelled out for us in the Sermon on the Mount, we must recognize the sin that lurks in our flesh and seeks to be satisfied. It is in direct contrast to the new life that God re-created us to live in Jesus. We must do anything necessary to avoid giving way to the desires of the flesh.

Why? Because God will indeed punish these sins: "The Lord is an avenger in all these things" (1 Thess. 4:6). God did not call us to impurity but to a holy life, and He has good reason to discipline and judge these kinds of sins: first, because they are not like Him, and second, they are not good for us.

When we reject God's commandment to be sanctified, we reject the resident power of the Holy Spirit, who is in us precisely to remind and empower us to live differently: "Whoever disregards this, disregards not man but God, who gives his Holy Spirit to you" (1 Thess. 4:8).

Remember the words of Peter:

Make every effort to be found spotless, blameless and at peace with him. Bear in mind that our Lord's patience means salvation, just as our dear brother Paul also wrote you with the wisdom that God gave him. He writes the same way in all his letters, speaking in them of these matters. His letters contain some things that are hard to understand, which ignorant and unstable people distort, as they do the other Scriptures, to their own destruction. Therefore, dear friends, since you have been forewarned, be on your guard so that you may not be carried away by the error of the lawless and fall from your secure position. But grow in the grace and knowledge of our Lord and Savior Jesus Christ. To him be glory both now and forever! Amen. (2 Pet. 3:14–18, NIV)

The Christian walk is to exude life, but that life demands discipline. Dallas Willard succinctly encapsulates this thought: "The need for discipline does not change when we come to all that is involved in walking in the holiness and power of Christ. Would we do the things that Jesus himself did and taught? Then there is a way. It is the way of disciplined grace: discipline under grace and grace in the midst of discipline."[2]

chapter 20

RETURNING TO DIVINE DESIGN

We truly live in a global village today. The rapid proliferation of media in all its forms has made for an accessibility of ideas and thoughts never considered possible by past generations. With it have come uninvited invasions of ideas hostile to biblical truth. Such opposition to the gospel is not new, but the ease with which it now travels from one continent to another is indeed stunning.

Too often believers have been unprepared to deal with this antagonism and in turn have allowed unbiblical teaching to affect the church. This problem is not limited to certain geographical locations. Whether or not we have had accessibility to books, teachers, and sound theological training, the easy and often uninvited entrance of teaching parading as biblical truth has had damaging results in the church at large.

Because of our failure to understand divine design—the life that God created us to live as transformed believers re-created in His image representing Him in our scattered marketplaces, cities, and nations—the church has too often focused on secondary matters and missed our primary calling. We have prioritized ministry, church, success, marriage, and family above God Himself. Because of this, we have a weak practical view of Scripture. This has led to the widespread habit of not spending time with God each day and letting the Holy Spirit direct us through His Word. The final result is that many of us have not engaged people around us with a God-focused, biblically consistent, transformationally expectant gospel.

These spiritual weaknesses have invaded the global Christian experience, and they threaten to produce nominal Christians everywhere as they challenge true biblical faith in so many unprepared to deal with them. If we intend to live out the calling God designed for His people and see the gospel reach men and women throughout the world, the church at large and every individual believer must return to divine design. After all, whatever God is going to do in the world, He is going to do primarily through all Christ's people.

God Alone Must Be Our Focus

Too often we are susceptible to error because we have allowed things other than God to consume our focus. But as we have noted throughout this book, the message of Genesis 1–3 leaves no room for vacillation as to God's design for our lives: we are created by God and for God, and as such we are created for relationship with Him and representation of Him in this world that He has given us to live in. This means that even good things like ministry, church, success, marriage, and family must never take the place of God's primary design for our lives.

One Bible teacher paints a beautiful picture of our relationship to God:

> The Savior simply reminds us of an invisible fact, our sonship to our Heavenly Father, who cares for and guides our lives. That is the fact which is completely sufficient to give all needful encouragement, to control our waywardness, to clear our vision for the true perspective, and to quicken us with an infinite aspiration, fresh, buoyant, and eternal.[1]

The industrial, technological, rationalistic world around us works to deceive us into believing that this world is all there is and therefore to be pursued and enjoyed at all costs. But God clearly contradicts this distorted position in His Word, calling us instead to eternal life in Christ:

> *I have been crucified with Christ. It is no longer I who live, but Christ who lives in me. And the life I now live in the flesh I live by faith in the Son of God, who loved me and gave himself for me (Gal. 2:20).*

> *I call heaven and earth to witness against you today, that I have set before you life and death, blessing and curse. Therefore choose life, that you and your offspring may live, loving the Lord your God, obeying his voice and holding fast to him, for he is your life and length of days. (Deut. 30:19–20)*

As Christians, we must constantly remember that we are a double creation of God. First, through His creation of Adam and Eve, God set His image and nature into all their children who would follow in succeeding generations. Then, in Jesus Christ, the Savior prepared before the foundation of the world, God redeemed us through the salvation achieved in Christ's death, burial, and resurrection, re-creating us in anticipation of that time in eternity when God's design for us will be fully restored.

The fullness God designed for His children in this world is discovered only in God's answer to man's two original questions: who am I? and, why do I exist? Everything we long for is found not in the pursuit of ministry, church, marriage, family, or some other good thing but in embracing relationship with God and representation of God in this world by who we are becoming and what we do with the many assets He has placed in our hands. All of our pursuits must be seen from this posture, or they will become confusing, frustrating, fruitless, and empty.

The Bible Must Be Our Rule of Faith and Life

I am amazed that so many Christians struggle with the obvious truth that Scripture must be our rule of faith and practice. Without a doubt their conviction of this fact has been eroded by a shallowness in their original confession coupled with the onslaught of the world from every side. Many might sheepishly say that they believe the Bible is inspired but would wonder what is meant by "rule of faith and practice." But if the Bible is inspired, or God-breathed, and if it contains as much of the story of life as we need to live fully with God and for Him, then it must also contain the answers, direction, and guideposts for everything we will encounter in life.

As we noted in chapter 3 of this book, John Bengel gave us a clear warning of our need to prioritize the Word of God:

Scripture is the foundation of the Church: the Church is the guardian of Scripture. When the Church is in strong health, the light of Scripture shines bright; when the Church is sick, Scripture is corroded by neglect; and thus it happens, that the outward form of Scripture and that of the Church, usually seem to exhibit simultaneously with either health or else sickness; and as a rule the way in which Scripture is being treated is in exact correspondence with the condition of the Church.[2]

Pascal gives further admonition for us to be often in God's Word:

Devotional reading is the readiness to leave all initiative in God's hands, to receive and wonder at what God has already done, and to be united with God in living and dynamic ways.[3]

The Bible is the language of the Holy Spirit. The more time we spend in it, the more we clean out the pores of our spiritual lives and are able to hear the whisperings of the Holy Spirit giving us direction and courage for every day. The Holy Spirit will not speak to us outside the language of Scripture.

When we engage with the inspired Word of God by the Holy Spirit, we have available to us all that we need to live to the glory of God and in the image of Jesus Christ. Without the Word we run the risk of being "tossed to and fro by the waves and carried about by every wind of doctrine, by human cunning, by craftiness in deceitful schemes" (Eph. 4:14).

We Must Embrace Intimacy with God

What makes intimacy with God so hard for us? Primarily the incorrect way some of us were brought to God. Did we accept Christ to escape from hell, to gain the promise of heaven, or to have all life's issues quickly resolved? These are not what salvation is all about in the Bible.

The full and guiding story about God and His mission as begun in Genesis 1–3 needs to be restored to our presentation of the gospel and understood by all Jesus followers. The clear offer from Scripture is restoration to relationship with God and representation of God. If a person does not want relationship with God and does not want to live a life that represents Him, that person does not want the gospel!

Jesus makes this quite clear: We are to love the Lord our God with all our hearts, minds, and souls and love our neighbor as ourselves. In the parable about the Samaritan, He further makes clear that our neighbor is much more than the person who lives next to us but includes everyone God brings across our path.

As a young man thoroughly instructed in the truths of the Scripture, I had to come to the discovery that although the truth is extremely important, it is given to lead us to the truth giver—Jesus Christ. To catch the truth but miss the giver of truth is to miss the essence of the gospel and the radical transformation that God offers us in Jesus Christ.

Why is intimacy with God so important? Because when we come into intimacy with God through salvation in Christ, He gives us a new nature! "Be perfect, as your heavenly Father is perfect" (Matt. 5:48) is possible only if we have been re-created with the nature of the Father within us. In Jesus Christ we have the seed of God planted within us, and we can be like our Father—more every day.

Jesus' statement that we are to be perfect is not a threat; it is a promise. We are created to be like our Father, and we can, because we now have His nature living in us. In Hebrews 4:16 we see that God is prepared to effect healing in us throughout our lives as we draw near to His throne of grace, and thus our lives will be in conformity to His righteousness and to the life we see in Jesus Christ.

So how do we facilitate intimacy with God? First, we need to spend some time every day, some way, listening to God in His Word. This time sets in our minds and our hearts the priority of life as He designed and desires it for us. Without God's thoughts regularly placed in our minds and taking precedence over our own, we are left to thoughts that arise from our flesh, from the world around us, or even from the enemy.

We also need extended time at some point every week with God in His Word. Times of extended refreshing with God reinforce and extend our daily times. We come away from these extended times reminded not only of our relationship to God but having had the opportunity to evaluate our representation of Him. As we reevaluate, we can adjust our commitments, release more assets, and be more in tune with the kingdom that is to come.

It is also good to spend a half day or more once every month or two in quietness, alone with God's Word before us. This keeps life in perspective, gives the Holy Spirit time to reorient our desires, and enriches all our other relationships. It helps us to more fully take control of our lives and give them to the Lord.

In these monthly or bi-monthly times, it is helpful to use more than one tool to take in and meditate on the things of God. Occasionally read a book by a believer who has finished his earthly course. A warning though: don't use radio, DVDs, music, or audio sermons as a substitute for personal time with God in His Word. These tools, while good on an occasional basis, are no substitute for hearing from God directly in Scripture. We need to hear God's voice in His Word and from His Spirit who lives in us. That is where the priesthood of the believer starts!

What will result from these spiritual disciplines? Dallas Willard says,

> The disciplines are activities of mind and body purposefully undertaken, to bring our personality and total being into effective cooperation with the divine order. They enable us more and more to live in a power that is, strictly speaking, beyond us, deriving from the spiritual realm itself, as we "yield ourselves to God, as those alive from the dead, and our members as instruments of righteousness unto God," as Romans 6:13 puts it.[4]

We Must Aggressively Engage People with the True Gospel

Too often believers think that it's the job of church leaders or missionaries to take the gospel to the world. But as people re-created in the image of God, made for relationship with God and representation of Him, every one of us is called by God to be on mission with Him, deliberately and aggressively taking the gospel to those in the marketplaces around us.

Not only that, but we must understand and thus present the gospel accurately. Our presentation of the gospel must be God focused, meaning that we share the Bible as the story of God acting unilaterally to offer mercy in Jesus through the Spirit so that people once created in His image can be restored to His original design. It must be biblically consistent, meaning that the message is a true reflection of the whole message of Scripture and not a truncated, redacted version built from extracted biblical texts or human experience. And it must be transformationally expectant, meaning that we understand and expect that salvation will anticipate transformation of men and women into the righteousness of God, especially as seen in the life of Jesus.

The Bible is one story running from Genesis to Revelation. It is in the beginning, in Genesis 1–3, that we see most clearly the divine design, and from that design all the other questions that we read about in the Bible are answered. From one point of view, most of Scripture contains explanatory, preparatory, and corroborating subplots of the primary story found at the beginning of Genesis. In order to fully appreciate what God has done and is doing throughout Scripture and throughout history, one must constantly move back and forth through God's Word between the beginning of the story and its many subplots. The fact that the story opens with creation is of eternal significance.

Genesis 1 is the starting point of the story and Revelation 22 the end. In between is the story, traced across human history, of how God Himself is accomplishing His purpose. Nothing in all creation bears the uniqueness of the human creation—not the animals, not the natural, not even the angels. God uniquely created Adam and Eve in His image and likeness, and by extension their offspring, for two bold purposes: to live in relationship to God and to represent God. This is the calling of the Bible—to be reconciled to God and His purposes in creating us.

The gospel cannot be extracted from this macro view. When it is, it minimizes the full extent of God's work and purpose and so leads to nominal Christians—people who appear to act on the offer of salvation but actually short-circuit the full and miraculous work that God has achieved in the death, burial, and resurrection of Jesus Christ. Such people say that they belong to Jesus but never look or act like Him.

The only way for men and women to look like Jesus is to follow Him into death, burial, and resurrection so that our original relationship to God and His purpose for our lives can be restored. Our old lawless man must be killed with Jesus on the cross and our new righteous man resurrected with Him. A person who has undergone this death, burial, and resurrection with Jesus Christ is now re-created and able to live for God.

The affirmation of the apostle John at the end of his life encapsulates this divine design of God: "To him who loves us and has freed us from our sins by his blood and has made us to be a kingdom and priests to serve his God and Father—to him be glory and power forever and ever! Amen" (Rev. 1:5–6, NIV). As believers in Jesus Christ created and re-created in the image of God, able to have relationship with Him and called to represent Him in this world, let us refocus on God, value His Word, embrace daily intimacy with the Lord, and live vibrant incarnational lives in the various places where He calls each one of us.

AFTERWORD

God has re-created us to be His righteous children in Jesus Christ. As we saw in this book, Jesus described in the Sermon on the Mount just how upside down this new life is meant to be in confession as well as living.

I wrote in the preface that I would not make this book story based. But I would be remiss if I did not give a few applications to the arguments that I have attempted to present.

Many years ago in his book *The Golden Cow*, author John White used strong language to describe his discovery that his mother was a whore. He was referring to the Western church and how it handled mammon, or money. He felt that the way in which Christians handled their assets was a travesty to the stewardship of God's wealth and goodness to them. Believers had not only kept too much "support" to themselves and housed themselves in earthly tents far exceeding their needs but had become stingy as well—stingy with what already belonged to God and what they were called to simply steward.

Os Guinness, in his book *Dining with the Devil*, written nearly twenty-five years ago but nonetheless highly germane to the church's present situation, asks some stark questions. One, do we really believe that the way the church does things today, focused as it is on structure and program, has no negative impact upon the kind of people it produces? And two, is outward worldly and fleshly success more important than what is happening inside those people who claim to be followers of Christ? As one contemporary pastor put it, we need to look at the scoreboard! In other words, how many are attending church, how much do they give, and are we all more or less happy?

Even the word "disciple," or "discipleship," has succumbed to mind-numbing corruptions. Too many consider good disciples as ones who adhere to religious program expectations, give their money to support the church's structure (oh, I'm sorry, I mean vision!), and, of course, confess the right doctrines (depending upon the denomination). Are we afraid to ask the question, "Is the church today being equipped?"

In Matthew 13:24–30, Jesus tells us the parable about the wheat and the tares, or weeds. The servant wanted to know if he was to harvest the tares from among the wheat. Instead the master instructed him to wait until the harvest time, and in the winnowing process, the tares would be eliminated. For many years I, like many others, have wondered how we can keep tares out of the church, and that is an appropriate concern. But today I am concerned that we may now actually have far more tares in the church than wheat. Our challenge is this: we must identify the people who truly belong to Christ and empower them to live in righteousness while making sure that we do not build our churches on and for the tares.

Jesus gave us His expectations for the church quite brusquely: "If you love me, you will keep my commandments" (John 14:15). This is exactly what I have attempted to point out in *Divine Design*. We were created and called for obedience. Anything less in our response to God is heresy. The really good news is that God the Spirit has come to grow us in this journey of obedience into righteousness, into the image of Jesus Christ.

Here are some ideas and examples of what obedience to God will look like in churches and in individual Christ followers.

First, in churches:

1. They would realize and repent of continuing to gather people in a service called "church" while knowingly seeing little to no Holy Spirit fruit in too many of their people.

2. They would begin to measure themselves not by external definitions of success but by whether their people are really and measurably growing to look more like Jesus every year.

3. They would repent of giving people what they want just to keep them coming and giving.

4. They would prioritize the priesthood (see 1 Pet. 2:9) that is to be practiced every day by every believer.

5. They would reject words and structures that allow people to substitute the pastor as their new priest.

6. They would build structures that demand dramatically fewer staff and more "ordinary" people using their gifts, unpaid, to serve the whole body.

7. They would repent of the obnoxious amount of money that the church corporately spends on itself, especially in its buildings.

8. They would give away much more of their budget to widows, orphans, the unprotected, and to ministries that measurably show that they know how to win people to Christ, organize them into local bodies, and grow them in the faith, anywhere and everywhere. Would giving away 50 percent of their income as a sign that they are under the stewardship of the Spirit be too much?

Second, in Christ followers:

1. We would find time to spend with God every day in His Word, no matter how busy life gets. There is no substitute for engaging with the most important relationship we have for

time and eternity, nor is there any excuse for neglecting it.

2. We would realize that as representatives of God, we hold His assets in our hands and thus cooperate with the Spirit to give them when, where, and to whom He indicates. Would giving away larger portions of our assets be wrong?

3. We would seek out and join churches that challenge and provide for us to live in daily obedience to God and His mercy mission.

4. We would study the concept of hospitality in the New Testament and discover that it is so much more than simply having people over for dinner. We should open our lives and our homes to widows, orphans, and unprotected people.

5. We would attend churches that challenge us to live the principles outlined above and have leaders who model it in their own lives, and we would avoid churches that are led by people we cannot intimately know and thus leave us with no idea what they do with their assets. We would avoid churches in which the leadership is clearly not living with their hands open.

6. We would be cautious about churches that spend more than 50 percent of their income from us, their members, on themselves: programs, building, and personnel. If a church cannot discipline itself to live the same kind of sacrifice they call us to show, we should be cautious.

7. We would seek out ways in which our marriages can be interdependent expressions of the uniqueness of our unions and of God's glory. We would seek out tangible ways for each spouse to encourage the faith and gifts of the other as well as ways those gifts can be invested in together.

A Final, Final Thought!

Over the years I have become increasingly convinced that Christ's people and their local gatherings are God's genius and the first line of expression of His glory and His desires. They are, by geography, embedded into the communities where God wants to expose His mercy message. They are within walking distance of any and all people whom God the Spirit is calling to salvation in their neighborhood. They are the incarnation of the reality that the grave is indeed empty as their lives progressively grow to demonstrate Christ's righteousness. They are God's salt and light and His hands to touch the unprotected around them. And in nations that have large numbers of Jesus followers, scattered across the cities and states of a nation, these believers make the gospel truly accessible to every man, woman, and child in their place when they live Christ's life in the midst of every small demographic of people.

We are inspired to hear of thousands of orphans being housed and fed, of millions of people gaining access to water. While I am not advocating the elimination of groups that work in this way nor their large strategies (and costly actions), I am more convinced that the real work that God has designed to be done in every small area of geography is best done by His local body, no matter how small that body may be. God's people working in this way will, in all probability, not change the systemic issues of their places. But they will transform the way people have an opportunity to think about the God of the Bible. And they will more completely fulfill God's design for the people in that community. As I said in the very first statement of this book, whatever God is going to do in the world, He is going to do primarily through all Christ's (local and accessible) people.

A number of years ago, I took this growing conviction and presented it to leaders with whom my ministry, Saturation Church Planting International, works in a particular nation. I challenged them to discover every human experience that was in their locality and then develop strategies to release their people into all of them, or at least into the ones that they and the Holy Spirit knew that they could handle.

They took up this challenge, and this last year they have seen God mobilize their people in extraordinary ways to win great numbers to

Christ, organize the new believers into new fellowships, and launch them on the journey of obedience to the Spirit (that is to say, these Christ followers have not merely shuffled people from one place to another and then called that a church plant). And, at the same time, they have:

1. Identified enslaved people in their midst, successfully taken steps to rescue them, and establish them in a new life
2. Found orphans in their midst and converted their own homes into sanctuaries for these unprotected ones
3. Fed the hungry and provided better water for the most destitute while also putting new roofs on their houses to protect them from the weather
4. Educated the outcast
5. Rescued the sexually enslaved and helped them build new lives

The numbers are not great in any of these examples. But the power of the example is that is shows what happens when local believers take the lost in their small locality serious, release their people to live the incarnation of the gospel in their communities, and open their own hands to spend the assets of God on other people. Ultimately, the cumulative power of this example can be seen when thousands of such local bodies do the same.

John wrote of this lifestyle: "By this all people will know that you are my disciples, if you have love for one another" (John 13:35). But what is love? Is it a good feeling about something or someone? Is its leading edge emotional? Is it a good relationship with another person? "Hey, I like being with you; let's be friends." Not in this case. Throughout the New Testament this word "love" appears again and again. But just as the Sermon on the Mount turns everything upside down, so too this love (*agape*) turns everything upside down. Its definition is simple but its application is profound. To love, in this sense, is to give your life for someone else. This is what Jesus did: He gave His life in exchange for ours. Of course, our giving does not carry the weight of eternal salvation weight, as His did. But it does extend His presence in the world as we take on the self-giving nature of Jesus and the Father who sent Him.

Without a growing expression of this self-giving, there can be no true witness of Christ in the world, and the presence of inbred, covetous, arrogant, stingy churches that have neither desire nor instruction in this love should be no surprise to us. But where we see the nature of God imaged on men and women who have been re-birthed in Jesus Christ growing and flourishing, the gospel has the opportunity to take root as the Spirit of God does His work to see some of the children of Adam and Eve restored to God.

appendix

A CHALLENGE TO CHURCH LEADERS

Having been involved in church leadership for many years, I have been privileged to be around Christian ministries that many would call successful. I have been a part of planting churches, leading large churches, growing a missionary agency, building alliances of churches, and even serving in national movements in which thousands of churches were planted and millions of people confessed that they wanted salvation in Christ. I have no doubt that many good, even eternally good, things were accomplished in these works. But if a person does anything with age and experience, it would be deep and fundamental reflecting. As I have reflected upon these "successful" things in light of a maturing understanding of Scripture, I have become convinced of one very important truth: it does not matter what we as Christian leadership grow if we don't grow people of divine distinction!

Too many in church leadership today have taken on the mind-set described by Os Guinness:

It is worth pondering a New Yorker lament about what is lost in the brave, new "audience-driven" preaching of the day: "The preacher, instead of looking out upon the world, looks out upon public opinion, trying to find out what the public would like to hear. Then he tries his best to duplicate that, and bring his finished product into a marketplace in which others are trying to do the same. The public, turning to our culture to find out about the world, discovers there is nothing but its own reflection. The unexamined world, meanwhile, drifts blindly into the future."[1]

Jesus, in contrast to this way of thinking, tells us quite simply in the Sermon on the Mount what people of divine distinction are: "You are the salt of the earth" (Matt. 5:13). Believers don't have to do anything special to be used of God, for Christ followers have been re-created through Jesus (regenerated) by God to be salt. Jesus does not tell Christians "Be salt" but "You are the salt." Believers being salt is part of the divine design.

An inherent warning comes naturally with this design: "If salt has lost its taste, how shall its saltiness be restored? It is no longer good for anything except to be thrown out and trampled under people's feet." Or, to say it another way, if believers lose their saltiness, they will become useless to their design and will be treated (trampled) by men as irrelevant, or useless! The greatest dimension of relevancy for the church is the saltiness of its people as they are sprinkled into the entire world in which they walk.

People of divine distinction are imperative to the world not because they believe something unique or do something unique on Sundays but because this is how God created them to be. Again, Jesus describes this quite simply: "Be perfect, as your heavenly Father is perfect" (Matt. 5:48). What Jesus does not say here is equally important: He is not so much commanding His people to be perfect as He is calling them to be like the Father whose genes they now carry. Much of the rest of the Sermon on the Mount is indeed a call to act out the perfectness of the Father. But to call us to act like Him, the people in our churches must bear an inherent image of Him. And they do—first in Adam and now, more importantly, in the last Adam, Jesus.

When we as Christian leadership grow people of divine distinction, we fulfill our mandate! Again, the result of our carrying out this mandate is simply put by Jesus: "You are the light of the world" (Matt. 5:14). As believers grow in their likeness to Jesus, they glorify God and declare to the world their intimate connection to Him.

Our primary mandate as pastors, teachers, evangelists, and missionaries is not to win the world, plant churches, or build programs but rather to make the evangelization of every place possible through the people God has entrusted to us.

How do we measure that kind of success? How do we know when we are really doing this? I see six criteria in the Bible for measuring whether the people in our care are truly living lives of divine distinction.

Are People Growing in Their Priesthood?

The first criterion for measuring whether we as leadership are accomplishing what God has for His people is when a majority of people in the church body are taking baby steps toward their priesthood and growing in their first calling—to be related to God and then to represent Him.

This is the calling of the Bible—to be reconciled to God and to His purposes in creating us. Genesis 1 is the starting point of the story and Revelation 22 the end. In between is the story, traced across human history, of how God Himself is accomplishing His purpose. Nothing in the universe bears the uniqueness of the human creation. Not the animals, not the natural, not even the angels. Unlike everything else in the universe, God created Adam and Eve, and by extension their offspring, for two bold purposes: to be in relationship to Him and to represent Him.

This message, as we noted in chapter 1 of this book, is traced across the pages of the Bible. In the giving of the law, Moses wrote in Deuteronomy 6:4–5 of our relationship with God: "Hear, O Israel: The Lord our God, the Lord is one. You shall love the Lord your God with all your heart and with all your soul and with all your might." And in Leviticus 19:18 he wrote of our representation of God in this world: "Do not seek revenge or bear a grudge against anyone among your people, but love your neighbor as yourself. I am the Lord" (NIV).

Jesus asserted the same two principles: "You shall love the Lord your God with all your heart and with all your soul and with all your mind. This is the great and first commandment. And a second is like it: You shall love your neighbor as yourself. On these two commandments depend all the Law and the Prophets" (Matt. 22:37–40).

The apostle Paul also wrote of how our relationship with Christ will lead to our representation of Him:

> *If anyone is in Christ, he is a new creation. The old has passed away; behold, the new has come. All this is from God, who through Christ reconciled us to himself and gave us the ministry of reconciliation; that is, in Christ God was reconciling the world to himself, not counting their trespasses against them, and entrusting to us the message of reconciliation. Therefore, we are ambassadors for Christ, God making his appeal through us.*
> *(2 Cor. 5:17–20)*

The task then of the church and therefore the leadership of the church is to cooperate with this primary call of God and to so nurture His people that they are growing in a continual and deepening relationship with Him and then faithfully representing Him.

Key questions immediately arise: Have we created an environment in the life of the body that faithfully, continually, and effectively champions this reality? Have we put resources into people's hands that allow them to grow their relationship with God? Do the programs of our church knowingly or unknowingly substitute for people's personal pursuit of their relationship with God? Can people get on with their relationship with God without us, if need be?

Are People Telling and Living Their Grace Testimonies?

The second criterion for measuring whether we as leadership are accomplishing what God has for His people is when a majority of our people are taking baby steps toward telling their grace testimonies.

Every believer in Christ is being built into a new building—indeed, a temple in which God Himself lives. Within this structure all Christ's people display both the individuality (see 1 Cor. 6:19) and corporateness (see Eph. 2:20–21) of God's residency within them. In this new temple He is building, God fits each rock (individual person) where He wants it to be. This perfect fitting by God, the master builder, gives each of Christ's people the greatest potential to be grown by the Spirit— through God's Word and his or her individual place in the midst of the body of Christ—into the person He wants each one to be. At the same time, together as Christ's fullness in the world (see Eph. 1:23) in local churches and families, believers are sprinkled as rays of gospel lights in their neighborhoods and marketplaces throughout the world.

It is this sprinkling of people, families, and local churches in and throughout the world that the Spirit uses to add new rocks into Christ's body (see Acts 2:42–47). One day, when this ministry of the gospel, lived and spoken by the Spirit through each and every one of Christ's people, has its full and complete course, Christ will return (see Matt. 24:14). But in the meantime, the growing and maturing distinctiveness of each individual believer and the body of Christ living as a whole in the world around them allow God's gospel message in Jesus to go to every man, woman, and child as believers share their own testimonies of grace in the marketplaces in which God has placed them.

The grand yet simple purpose of this new design of God's is too often lost in the overly structured institution that so many today call the church. From Ephesians 3:10–11 we see that God has always intended that His people be the bearers of His gospel: "Through the church the manifold wisdom of God might now be made known to the rulers and authorities in the heavenly places. This was according to the eternal purpose that he has realized in Christ Jesus our Lord." In this passage we find five important realities.

First, God has only had one purpose from the very beginning. Paul emphasizes this singularity of God's purpose by choice of grammar—"His eternal purpose" being singular rather than plural. And while God's purpose was not clearly seen during Old Testament history (see Eph. 3:9), it has been working itself through history ever since Adam and Eve sinned. God's instrumentality and revelation grew and were preserved on the stage of time until, at just the right moment, Jesus came.

Second, for this time on Earth God has only one instrument: the church. Whatever God is going to do in the neighborhoods, cities, states, and even nations of the world, He is going to do through each and every one of Christ's people. None can be left out of the living and telling of the gospel story. The untraceable grace (see Eph. 3:8) of God's working in Christ will find particular, unique, exhaustive, and ultimately universal expression through each of Christ's people. He will tell His story of grace, now that Jesus is at God's right hand, through each of Christ's followers. No one is insignificant in this task. No one is dispensable!

Third, the purpose of this eternal plan, played out in history through so many in preparation of the coming of the Christ, is to fully release the grace story of the gospel. Paul says that "the manifold wisdom of God" is seen through the instrument—Christ's body, the church. I referred to this grace-telling ministry through the church in the previous paragraph as particular, unique, exhaustive, and ultimately universal. It is particular because every one of Christ's people has received it. It is unique because each one who has received it has received it in their own unique way; their story about it is like nobody else's story, which is why Paul calls it manifold. Every single story of how each Christ follower came to grace is another unique brush stroke on God's painting called grace. Without each of them it is incomplete, and with all of them it tells the whole story that God wants to tell. It is exhaustive because all the particular and unique stories will someday add up to the whole story. No sin will be greater than grace! And it is ultimately universal because it will be preached to the whole world, and then the end will come. People from every tribe, tongue, and nation will be transformed by it.

Fourth, this particular, unique, exhaustive, and universal display of the grace of God working through Christ's people is the eternal enigma to the unseen forces beyond time, inhabiting eternity—the "rulers and authorities in the heavenly places." Satan and his hordes don't understand grace, because they know us and our failings. But each of Christ's people individually, to say nothing of the corporate millions of them together as a body, is a particular, unique, exhaustive, and universal statement of the enigma of grace.

Fifth, this teaching of Paul's, received by revelation from the Lord, is not a momentary knee-jerk reaction by God in an attempt to rescue a good plan gone bad through sin. No, it conforms precisely to God's eternal order of things. Not only is God working this tangible demonstration of the story of grace through each and every one of Christ's people in time but for eternity as well.

In this passage in Ephesians, it is plain for us to see that the purpose of God's people is to live and share their testimonies of grace before a watching world! Christ's church is not a storehouse to gather people for preaching or even worship services; it is not a values club offering programs to train adult and child alike in good values; it is not a social club for us to discover good friends and fellowship.

People clamor for organizational structure to the church because they seek safety, and leadership complies with people's desires because they seek significance. The body of Christ does need structure, and people can have safety without sin, even while leaders can have significance without sin. But when structure leads to institution, and when people choose safety over God's purpose that they engage the world with the gospel through their grace testimonies, and when leaders choose institutional significance over divesting power into Christ's people to live out God's grace design, then the church has succumbed to sin. Worse, it has cut off the single-most important instrument besides the Holy Spirit that God has to engage the world with His grace message: people!

Are People Using Their Spiritual Gifts?

The third criterion for measuring whether we as leadership are accomplishing what God has for His people is when a majority of our people are taking baby steps toward using their spiritual gifts.

If the Spirit of God has sovereignly given to all Christ's people gifts by which to express their service to God, then it is unacceptable for them not to be growing in their understanding and use of them. Gifts are the energies of the Holy Spirit in us to enable us to give strategic expression to the many ministries that Jesus wants to work through His people. To lose the maturation of even one person as it pertains to their deployment in the church to the world is to diminish the creative genius that God has designed for His people.

First Corinthians 12 presents us a challenge on this matter. The picture painted by Paul of the body in this passage is only a metaphor, but it dominates the whole of the chapter, and as such has a significant message for the church today. In thinking about gifts and leadership, several universals apply.

Gifts are given to each and every one of Christ's people (see 1 Cor. 12:7). No follower is left without at least one Spirit-energized ability, and probably most Christians, if not all, have a mosaic of gifts. I speak of gifts as Spirit-energized abilities because they are more probably the Spirit Himself working through His people in different ways. This is a needed corrective to the idea that somehow these gifts belong to the individual believers who possess them. Christians do not possess their gifts; the gifts possess the believers, even as the Spirit lives in and through each one to accomplish that individual's personal and earthly ends in the ministry of the gospel and ultimately in the sovereign completion of God's designs over human history. The Holy Spirit does fully cooperate with people's personalities, but He does so in ways that move His power through them for God's ends, not their personal fulfillment. Yes, believers do feel fulfilled when they cooperate with such movement by the Spirit, but the giving is not for their personal fulfillment.

The gifts exist for the common good (see 1 Cor. 12:7). If there were no common good that God saw fit to be accomplished through individual gifting, orchestrated in and through the corporate body, then gifts would not be given. The gifts are not for Christ followers to possess, fondle, adore, or reject. They are for the common good of others and the purposes of God.

The gifts that believers receive are decided exclusively by the Spirit (see 1 Cor. 12:11). Christians do not decide which gifts they are given, nor do Christian parents decide which ones they would like their children to have. Theological training schools cannot guarantee that a person will receive the gifts that he deems most important. The Spirit, without people's consultation, decides by His sovereignty and for God's purposes which ones each person is to receive. Of course, in His wisdom of people's personal histories and personalities, He can be trusted to give gifts that will most cooperate with people's personal fulfillment and God's purposes.

The true effectiveness of the gifts, as they are played out through ministries, or "body parts," as Paul calls them, is measured in the cooperative and coordinative dance of the whole body together (see 1 Cor. 12:12–26). No body part can deny the validity of another, and no body part can think of itself as possessing the most important place in the configuration of parts. Indeed, we are left with this somewhat uncomfortable declaration by Paul that a healthy body does all that it can to both protect and honor the hidden and least publicly honorable parts of the body. A far cry from the man-at-the-top syndrome infecting the church today!

One last nuance needs identification before we close this short review of Spirit gifts. The Trinity cooperates together in the preparation of the body, and each part in the body, to fulfill its role in God's purposes (see 1 Cor. 12:4–6). The Spirit controls the distribution of gifts, Jesus the Son controls the ministries in which these gifts will operate, and God the Father controls the effects, or domains, as I call them, of the gifts and ministries. What is the purpose and meaning of this revelation?

Perhaps that God the Father, God the Son, and God the Holy Spirit are a model of the kind of cooperation and coordination that is expected from the people of Christ. It takes the cooperative and coordinated ministry by all three to fully empower, engage, and mobilize the body of Christ into its divinely ordained purpose.

I think all would agree that God the Father is the first among equals, as the Bible is replete with such indications as to the Father's role in the Trinity. But who would want to attribute to God the Father the likes of the man-at-the-top syndrome now controlling so much of Western Christianity? Surely the attitude of Jesus Himself is instructive in this regard: "Let Christ himself be your example as to what your attitude should be. For he, who had always been God by nature, did not cling to his prerogatives as God's equal, but stripped himself of all privilege" (Phil. 2:5–7, Phillips). The Trinity, in its own mysterious way, is actively cooperating together in the full capacitating of the body of Jesus to fulfill its role in the purposes of God.

Moreover, 1 Corinthians 12 indicates a much deeper diversity regarding each believer than that which pertains to the matter of gifts alone. If we would look at the words of this passage through the picture of a circle, we would see four pieces to that circle.

The first piece is the mosaic of gifts that God the Spirit has given to each Christ follower. It is reasonable to assume that the cluster each believer is given not only comes with the sovereign knowing of God of that person's place in the body and His purpose for him or her in that place but of the cooperative impact of these gifts in and through each individual.

The second piece is the differing ways in which each believer serves, or ministers, within the body of Christ and for the purposes of God. We find not only an infinite number of ways that people's gifts can be used but any number of ways, places, or ministries in which each one's personal mosaic of gifts can be used. In fact, the precise mix of people's gifts may change over their lifetimes, at least as to which of their gifts takes the lead.

The third piece is the energies, or impacts, that these gifts and their ministries have within the body of Christ and for the purposes of God—in other words, the domain, or breadth of influence, that the sovereign God determines each believer in Christ will have. Of course, ego, assertiveness, and aggression can also explain the breadth of some people's ministries; good marketing can supersede the designs of God. But when Christians cooperate with the work of the Trinity and in the ebb and flow of the other body parts, then God sovereignly puts each person in the place of influence He needs that individual to be in. Again, none of this is for the believer's own glory any more than any of a person's own body parts performs its function for its own glory! When we see this kind of active cooperation with the full-orbed ministry of the Trinity, we also see the desires of people's hearts, the full mobilization of Christ's people, and the full evangelization of the world fully met.

But there is one more piece needed to complete the circle, and it is the most mysterious. The fourth and final piece is people's own personalities. God has a gracious way of working in and through all His people in such a way as to highlight Himself and His purposes—not to turn people into His robots but to bring great joy and fulfillment to their lives. As the historic statement about inspiration so ably states (see 2 Tim. 3:16), God so worked in the authors of the Bible that, without destroying their own unique personalities, He communicated through them His own God-breathed Word.

In my own early days of serving the body of Christ in this ministry called leadership, I began to notice that many leaders did just the opposite, as I saw each successive man or group of men whom I worked under define the role of "leader" according to their own callings. For example, if I was working under a pastor (according to the function described in Ephesians 4:11), then he defined the role of leader or pastor or youth pastor with mercy overtones. For the mercy person, a good leader or pastor was supposed to invest significant portions of every day with people in such activities as hospital and home visitations.

When I worked for a managerially inclined leader, he projected "manager" over the definition of "leader" and, of course, expected the most desirable activities of a good manager. Thus I was expected to read books on management, learn to plan, and handle committee meetings and the work of colleagues.

The evangelist expected me to be a great soul winner. The pastor expected me to define my life by the compassionate engagement of Christ's people and their needs. The teacher expected me to spend long hours studying God's Word and to become the expert exegete that the Holy Scriptures deserved. The one who had the gift of exhortation expected me to be willing to spend long hours listening to and sympathizing with people's struggles. All of us are great at projecting our own gifts or functions on others!

It took years of reflection and dissatisfaction for me to come to my own personal understanding of God's wonderful and diverse working in each believer in ways that confirm us as unique to Him and useful for His purposes. Without hesitation I can joyfully affirm that I am not a manager, so I don't enjoy managing the things that good managers enjoy managing. I am not an evangelist, so I don't act like one. I am not a pastor, so compassion is not my first response to people's needs.

Yes, I have spent time reading in all these disciplines, and for good reasons. First, it helps me confirm who I am not. Second, it helps me appreciate the work that people who have these gifts do. Third, it reminds me of the importance of the diversity being woven into a unified whole for the important task of empowering Christ's people. Fourth, it teaches me how to practice the core issues in each gift that are expected from all Christ's people. From the pastor I learn to pursue compassion; from the evangelist I learn to share my witness; from the teacher I learn the importance and pursuit of truth. But none of these gifts or ministries or domains are mine.

The gifts that the Spirit of God works through me orbit around leading and preaching. Along with small pieces of other gifts, these comprise my spiritual-gifts mosaic. But these gifts can be used in multiple ways and can change over time. At times the gift of preaching dominated, and I was found primarily in a local church. At other times the gift of leading was stronger, and I was found in the leadership of a missions organization. At the present time, I see an interesting blend of both developing in a way that they never have before. I am fulfilling the function of a prophet and working in what I call an apostolic structure.

God the Spirit is working the gifts of leading and preaching through my life. God the Son is working to place me into the right place (body part) at the right time within the worldwide ministry of the gospel through the church. And God the Father is working the impact (domain) of all this as He knows is best. All this the Trinity does without destroying who I am or turning me into a mere robot.

Yes, believers are expected to submit to the perfecting work of the Holy Spirit and the Word of God. The more Christians, both those who are in leadership and "ordinary" believers, allow the Holy Spirit to work the effects of the resurrection into their lives, the more they will look qualitatively like the Master, Jesus, and, by extension, the more effective will be the ministry of the gospel through their gifts and domain.

Are People Maturing in the Fruit of the Spirit?

The fourth criterion for measuring whether we as leadership are accomplishing what God has for His people is when a majority of our people are taking baby steps toward maturing in the fruit of the Spirit.

This will be seen in the Spirit of God working the fruit of the Spirit in God's people in their relationships to each other and to the world. Paul lists these interpersonal qualities in Galatians 5:22–23: "The fruit of the Spirit is love, joy, peace, patience, kindness, goodness, faithfulness, gentleness, self-control." These characteristics are the natural result of the Holy Spirit living in Christ's people, and, as such, they ought to be growing in maturity and expression in each follower of Christ.

Individuals, marriages, families, and congregations growing in the fruit of the Spirit express the most powerful proof on Earth that the grave is empty and that Jesus lives in His people. Their growing expression of these otherwise enigmatic qualities demonstrate the uniqueness of the power that lives in each of them.

The expression of this fruit incarnated in Christ's people in the world around them has compelling force. This is the point of the words of James: "Religion that God our Father accepts as pure and faultless is this: to look after orphans and widows in their distress and to keep oneself from being polluted by the world" (Jas 1:27, NIV). The church, when it lives out the incarnation of its Master, has always been an enigma to the world. The world gives scant attention to those who are unprotected, but the church finds ways to include these people in their lives and, in fact, works diligently to bring healing to their brokenness. This is one of the most compelling foundations for the church's work of evangelism in the world.

I see nowhere in Scripture that the systemic problems of the world stemming from sin in man and his systems will necessarily be cured. But it is clear in God's Word that people trapped within the most heinous results of man's systems are to be individually touched, healed, and rescued. This is the power of the church around the world that I have been privileged to observe. It is now no surprise to find church-based orphanages, drug-rehab centers, and feeding programs in local churches diligently carrying out the Great Commission in their various places.

Local churches must be willing to champion and measure such interpersonal growth in their people lest they fall prey to accommodating crowds of people claiming to be on the road to heaven but living little of its calling. It is not hard for a willing local church to grow its people in the fruit of the Spirit, especially if they have almost any kind of small-group ministry in their body in which a majority of their people are involved. In such a scenario we should expect to see the incarnated fruit of the Spirit operating in the relationships of the people in the church as they forgive, forget, bear with, and love others within the body.

Not only that, but we should champion the church's calling to the cities and neighborhoods in which our congregations are situated and expect to see our people begin ministering to each and every subgroup of people around us. When this does not happen, something is desperately wrong!

Are People Stewarding Their Assets for the Extension of God's Kingdom?

The fifth criterion for measuring whether we as leadership are accomplishing what God has for His people is when a majority of our people are taking baby steps toward stewarding their assets for the kingdom of God.

Once a person has moved from death to life through crucifixion, burial, and resurrection with Jesus, his or her new heart is designed to put God at the center. God has not designed the new heart for sharing space with anything else. Money, however, as the most tangible thing belonging to the world system, wants expression—domination if it can have it. But Jesus, in Matthew 6:24, made clear, "You cannot serve God and money."

Where money finds expression in a person, a God-consciousness seems to be below the surface of their actions, which are often even religious and humane. But transformation is not present in such a person, for in the transformed heart God has designed only one occupant: Himself.

Where money finds domination in a person, God is not present in that individual at all. In such a case, any expression of human greed becomes possible. And as Jesus tells us in Matthew 6:23, if the light within a person is darkness, how great is that darkness!

From this posture the whole of Matthew 6:19–34 is understandable, especially as a beginning point for helping those in our care steward their lives here on Earth in light of the transformation that begins with the new birth.

Believers are not to store up for themselves treasures on Earth. We discussed six reasons for this in chapter 15 of this book, reasons that Jesus makes clear in the Sermon on the Mount. First, Christians are not to store up treasures on Earth because they will rot. The apostle John confirms this in 1 John 2:17: "The world is passing away along with its desires." Earthly treasures can disappear because of this world's corrupt systems of finance or because someone steals them or because they grow old and wear out, but in the end, possessions stored up in the world will not last.

Second, Christians are not to store up treasures on Earth because their relationship with God is focused on the eternity that He has designed. That eternity, which we currently know as heaven, is the only safe place for the believer's most cherished things.

The third reason Christians are not to store up treasures on Earth is because whatever dominates the heart owns the person. There is no sin inherent in created things, but when men use things to take the place of their Creator God, it is sin.

The fourth reason Christians are not to store up treasures on Earth is because when their hearts are focused on possessions, they are unable to see clearly. This leads to darkness and to all kinds of evil behavior.

Finally, Christians are not to store up treasures on Earth because they must choose between self and God. People cannot serve two opposing forces. God's new creation has only one occupant at its center: God Himself. Jesus understood that trusting God for physical provision could produce anxiety in His people, so He reminded them that the God who takes care of the birds and the fields does so with great concern and lavish beauty. And how much more valuable are God's people than birds? Our God can care for the needs of His people!

As we noted in chapter 15, the apostle Paul counseled Timothy on this matter:

Command those who are rich in this present world not to be arrogant nor to put their hope in wealth, which is so uncertain, but to put their hope in God, who richly provides us with everything for our enjoyment. Command them to do good, to be rich in good deeds, and to be generous and willing to share. In this way they will lay up treasure for themselves as a firm foundation for the coming age, so that they may take hold of the life that is truly life. (1 Tim. 6:17–19, NIV)

How can we help our churches combat the world's view regarding riches? First, by teaching them to focus on God's design for His children, which is the antithesis of the system we live in; second, by teaching them to nurture the God-designed life resident within them; and third, by teaching them to embrace God's gifts and enjoy them.

Paul goes on to define three ways in which God's people can invest the good things that come to them from the hand and provision of God. First, they are to be rich in good deeds; that is, Christians are to convert their treasures to the benefit of others. Second, they are to be generous—to give some of their treasure away. And third, they must be willing to share, assessing all the items God has given them—clothes, cars, houses, family, money—and sharing these items with those in need.

God expects His children, because of their new relationship to Him, to live with open hands and generous hearts, their eyes focused out on eternity, and their lives invested in the extension of the kingdom of God.

Are People Reducing the Number of Those Lost in Their Areas?

The sixth and final criterion for measuring whether we as leadership are accomplishing what God has for His people is when the believers who make up the local body are making a measurable impact on the number of those who are lost in the places in which they live.

The potential for leadership being personally deceived as we attempt to deliver empowerment to Christ's people is strong. Many leaders today have such a weak and incomplete theology of church that they are lulled into believing that what goes on in a building or program is a valid measurement of their effectiveness, both in Christ's people and in the world. This delusion casts its spell over people and leaders alike, causing leaders to sincerely believe that if their church is adding people or is simply content or is Spirit-filled or is—you fill in the blank!—then they are accomplishing their purpose. Indeed, they believe they are a model for others to emulate!

I learned early on in ministry that I needed to make a strategic application of my biblical convictions about church so that I avoid deceiving myself into thinking that something was happening in the church when in reality nothing more than herd psychology and warehousing was going on. I have come to call this strategic application "circle accountability."

Circle accountability is asking God the Holy Spirit to give our local church a geographical sphere around us where we can empower and mobilize all our resources in such a way as to guarantee that in a specific timeframe every man, woman, and child in our area can have the opportunity to hear, understand, and accept or reject Jesus as Savior. It also seeks to have those coming to faith in Him incorporated into the life of a local church that (1) empowers them to practice their own priesthood and grow in intimacy with the heavenly Father, (2) empowers them and holds them accountable to tell their particular and unique story of grace in all the relationships that the Spirit of God has given to them, and (3) provides the environment for them to identify their Spirit-giftedness and empowers them to use their gifts in the church and, most importantly, in the world where they spend the majority of their time.

Circle accountability is the direct opposite of the theology of church that I inherited. My early thinking measured the church's effectiveness by what I call inside-out thinking—in essence, measuring ourselves to ourselves and feeling satisfied, safe, and even smug sometimes. No matter what spiritual terms we used, my church's real effectiveness was measured by whether we got bigger or not. Where the people attending our church came from and what they were doing with their faith, both in their families and in their relationships, was in effect secondary to us.

Outside-in thinking, on the other hand, causes us to reference ourselves to the gospel purpose of the church in the midst of the whole community in which we live and in cooperation with the broader body of Christ in that same community. "Is the gospel being measurably delivered to our community?" becomes the core question. And that is a question that is easy to measure!

What Makes These Criteria So Difficult for Leaders?

If these six criteria provide the litmus test of biblical leadership, what makes them so difficult for us to live them out in our churches and ministries?

First, our historical theology about the church is erroneous. For generations many Christians have defined church as a place to gather rather than as a people to be grown in the practices of faith and participation in the ministry of the purpose of the church.

Second, our own egos get in the way! It is easy to see why the gathered church has so much personal meaning for those who lead it, especially if they have been able to collect many people. Those people learn to "love" their leaders, appreciate them, and shower them with significance and even financial benefit. But when we are truly driven by the empowerment mandate given by Jesus to those who lead His church, then our desire for significance will give way to our personal, daily, and intimate relationship with God. Leaders are to be merely midwives to help God's people live the truth in meaningful relationship to the giver of truth! In this posture, leadership does indeed decrease, for Christ must increase.

Third, the great majority of people in the church today, through our leadership, have become entrenched in expectations based upon an erroneous idea of the church and their involvement in its purpose. They do not expect much of anything that defines the early church. They have come to expect that the leadership will do anything and everything to make it possible and desirable for them to be in our church. Through our parking structures, buildings, programs, and other benefits, we have taught them that church is indeed all about them. We have cooperated with, and in many cases exacerbated, the inherent narcissism of man and the growing self-centeredness of our culture.

To now call our people to act in light of the words of Jesus, or even to act at all, will require a long road of re-evangelizing many who are not just nominal but not believers at all, reeducating many of them that the faith as they understood it was misrepresented by us and reshaping all of them to put their daily relationship with God at the center of their lives.

The church and its leaders today are in need of reformation! A re-programming of the old idea of church as a place where people go will not do. We are in desperate need of questioning not what we do but the way in which we think!

This generation of church must make a journey focused on how we think before we decide what to do, a journey that will demand beliefs that are in antithesis to the easy answers abounding in the Christian world of today. It will demand time and reflection. It will lead to correction.

NOTES

Introduction: God's Mission—and Our Place in It

1. When I mention "marketplaces" I am referring mostly to the places in which Christians work. However, the marketplace is not limited to a Christian's place of work but includes the totality of where he spends his time—where he works, shops, works out, spends his free time. Perhaps a clearer term is "circle of accountability." This refers to all the unbelievers whom God has placed in a Christian's life for whom he is responsible for sharing the gospel. Whatever we call the place where we live, the fact is that wherever we encounter people in our everyday lives and routines, we are to represent and display Christ.

2. We have detailed this sequence on the church in Ephesians more fully in a book titled *Renovation: Divine Design in the Life of the Church*, available at www.scpglobal.org.

Chapter 1: Divine Design Revealed

1. Erich Sauer, *The Dawn of World Redemption* (Grand Rapids: Eerdmans, 1953), 1:2, http://www.worldinvisible.com/library/sauer/dawnredm/dwrtable.htm (accessed May 16, 2016).

2. Ibid., 2:1.

3. I have written more complete and detailed thoughts on the

idea of interdependency, especially in church leadership, in a book titled *Alone at the Top*. This resource is available for purchase at http://scpglobal.org/resources/.

4. Todd Charles Wood, "Fellowship, Creation, and Schistosomes," Institute for Creation Research, January 1, 2003, http://www.icr.org/article/fellowship-creation-schistosomes/(accessed April 14, 2016).

5. Blaise Pascal, *Pensees* (Paris: 1669), chap. 5, thought 583, http://www.ccel.org/ccel/pascal/pensees.i.html (accessed May 16, 2016).

6. Abraham Kuyper, "The Work of the Holy Spirit Distinguished" in *Work of the Holy Spirit* (1900), 21.

7. Os Guinness, *The Call: Finding and Fulfilling the Central Purpose of Your Life* (Nashville: W Publishing Group, 1998), 31.

Chapter 2: Created—and Re-created—in the Image of God

1. Walter Kaiser, *Toward an Exegetical Theology* (Grand Rapids: Baker, 1981), 33–34.

2. C. S. Lewis in Clyde S. Kilby ed., *A Mind Awake: An Anthology of C. S. Lewis* (New York: Harcourt Brace, 1968), 105.

Chapter 3: Cultivating Relationship with God

1. John Bengel in Kaiser, *Toward an Exegetical Theology*, 7.

Chapter 4: Representing God in the World

1. Guinness, *The Call*, 69–70.

2. F. F. Bruce, *The Epistle to the Hebrews* (Grand Rapids: Eerdmans, 1964), 23.

Chapter 5: Heirs Together of the Gracious Gift of Life

1. Randy Alcorn, *Heaven* (Carol Stream, IL: Tyndale, 2004), 349.

Chapter 8: Relationship Leads to Representation

1. Andrew Murray, *Working for God, Christian Classics Ethereal Library* (New York: Revell, 1901), http://www.ccel.org/ccel/murray/working.html (accessed April 18, 2016).
2. Kenneth Latourette, *A History of Christianity* (New York: Harper & Brothers, 1953), 21.
3. Dallas Willard, "Rethinking Evangelism," Dallas Willard, winter 2001, http://www.dwillard.org/articles/artview.asp?artID=53 (accessed April 18, 2016).
4. Philip H. Towner, *1–2 Timothy & Titus* (Downers Grove, IL: InterVarsity Press, 1994), 247–48.

Chapter 10: Righteousness vs. Anger

1. Charles H. Mackintosh, "The Bible: Its Sufficiency and Supremacy," *Things New and Old*, vol. 5 (London: 1862).

Chapter 11: Purity vs. Lust

1. Lewis, *A Mind Awake*, 193.
2. G. K. Chesterton, *The Everlasting Man* (Vancouver, BC: Regent College Publishing, 2006), 185.

Chapter 12: Truth and Love vs. Oaths and Revenge

1. *The Confessions of Saint Augustine* (New York: Doubleday, 1960), 355.

Chapter 13: Giving to the Needy

1. Dietrich Bonhoeffer, *The Cost of Discipleship* (New York: Touchstone, 1995), 334.
2. Albert Barnes, *Notes, Explanatory and Practical, on the Epistles of Paul: to the Thessalonians, to Timothy, to Titus, and to Philemon* (Ulan, 2014), 232.

Chapter 14: Praying and Fasting

1. Pascal, *The Mind on Fire* (Colorado Springs: Cook, 2006), 163.
2. Augustine, *On the Lord's Sermon on the Mount*, 2:3:14.

Chapter 15: Keeping Our Treasures in Heaven

1. Guinness, *The Call*, 131.
2. Ibid., 133–34.

Chapter 16: Letting God Be the Judge

1. Jamieson, Fausset, and Brown, *Whole Bible Commentary*, commentary on Matthew 7:1, http://www.biblestudytools.com/commentaries/jamieson-fausset-brown/matthew/matthew-7.html (accessed May 24, 2016).

Chapter 17: Seeking God and Loving Others

1. Oswald Chambers, "The Spiritually Lazy Saint" (entry for July 10) in *My Utmost for His Highest* (Grand Rapids: Discovery, 2010).

Chapter 18: Watching Out for Deception

1. Mackintosh, "The Bible: Its Sufficiency and Supremacy."

Chapter 19: Living in Order to Please God

1. William Wilberforce, *Real Christianity* (Ventura, CA: Regal, 2006), 69.

2. Willard, "Live Life to the Full," Dallas Willard, April 14, 2001, http://www.dwillard.org/articles/artview.asp?artID=5 (accessed April 18, 2016).

Chapter 20: Returning to Divine Design

1. Rev. E. Lyttelton, *Studies in the Sermon on the Mount* (Charleston, SC: BiblioBazaar, 2009), 34.

2. Bengel in Kaiser, *Toward an Exegetical Theology*, 7.

3. Pascal, *The Mind on Fire*, 299.

4. Willard, *The Spirit of the Disciplines: Understanding How God Changes Lives* (New York: HarperOne, 1990), 68.

Appendix: A Challenge to Church Leaders

1. Guinness, *Dining with the Devil: The Megachurch Movement Flirts with Modernity* (Grand Rapids: Baker, 1993), 59.